Captured at the Battle of the Bulge

Captured at the Battle of the Bulge

Memoir of a P.O.W.

Sgt. E. Russell Lang

Personal History Press
Lincoln, Massachusetts

ISBN 978-0-9983619-0-1

Library of Congress Control Number: 2015936813

The author and the publisher gratefully acknowledge the generous assistance of Carl Wouters for making the maps on pages 37, 40, 42, and 66, and for his service as the 106th Association Belgian Liaison.

PHP
Personal History Press
59 South Great Road
Lincoln, Massachusetts 01773

Table of Contents

Illustrations

Illustrations continued

Russ Lang

Russ was born August 1, 1921. He grew up in Torrington, Connecticut. This photo was taken in Marlboro, Massachusetts, March 2015.

Introduction

The following memoirs are my best attempt of recalling a part of my life when I responded to my country's call. I started this effort as a result of my son Russell's request to me to transcribe a fading penciled note book. It was my diary, written during my time as a World War II prisoner of war.

After completing the diary I anticipated some of the questions that may be asked someday. How did this happen, where were you when?—and so on. So chapters were continually added, fore and aft, until it progressed into what covered my memory of all of the World War II years. I must emphasize that not all of the information written here is absolute. It is the best of what was in my memory, the memories of other veterans and the research done in books. When engaged in combat, you are only aware of what is happening in your immediate area. When subjected to enemy fire, the confusion and the stress that surrounds you affects what you chose to forget or remember. We on the front line seldom knew the Army's final objective, didn't know what was happening to the units next to us or even knew what we accomplished until much later on. As the battle rages, the battle plan may change as the units meet overpowering resistance or new opportunities open up to them. While I recorded these events of my past, I too had many questions that drove me in search for answers. I also became aware that I sometimes assumed what had taken place. With the help of a West Point colonel who provided me with the text and maps of the official history of the Battle of the Bulge and using other texts as well, I was able to fill in the gaps. The Internet connected me to John Kline of the 106th Infantry Division Association and then to the many Company I veterans who shared their memories with me. I believe that I have now recorded an accurate account of my experiences.

Writing this journal also opened up some new doors for me. I have been able to reunite with some of those POWs who were in my company and who also shared in some of these events. They have helped me put some old ghosts to rest. A few of the historians were unkind and quick to deride the efforts of the

106th Infantry Division in the Battle of the Bulge. They did not take the time to get all of the facts. Much like when I started to record these memoirs, they made some assumptions in their writings. They caused many veterans of the 106th to carry undeserved shame for being a POW. Accounts that are available now show that large mistakes and events that were outside the control of the 106th Division caused its two regiments to surrender.

The 2nd Division Commander, the division that we replaced in the line, had requested a change in the positions we occupied because they were indefensible. His request was denied. An air-drop of supplies from England was never dropped because of a communication error in the Air Corps. A 7th Armored unit that was only a few kilometers away received orders to support these two regiments. The counter attack was canceled. It could have changed the outcome of the battle being fought by these trapped men. It still isn't clear why or who made this decision. I knew what condition my company was in so I knew Col. Cavender must have had no alternative but to surrender. German accounts later stated that the stubborn resistance of the 106th upset their time table and gave St. Vith and Bastone three more days to prepare its defenses. I now have an even greater respect and pride of my company and regiment's record. I understand its contribution to the outcome of the Battle of the Bulge that became the start of the final destruction of the German forces on the Western Front.

E. Russell Lang
October 25, 2000

Chapter One

Pearl Harbor

When Pearl Harbor was bombed by the Japanese on Sunday, December 7, 1941, I was living at home in Torrington, Connecticut, with my mother and father. Around 1:00 p.m. the music of the Sammy Kaye orchestra on the radio was interrupted by the news of the attack. When the news broadcast was over, I went for a walk alone through my favorite woods off the Torringford Road. I was angry that our country was attacked but felt that the Japs must be crazy to think that they could have a chance of winning a war against us. As the days went on, Hitler and the Axis powers became involved and now we were at war with all of them. We were in a World War and now I wondered what would become of my future.

I was an apprentice tool and die maker at the Union Hardware Company. Our company made roller and ice skates, sporting goods, and hardware tools. When war was declared everything was to be utilized: people, materials and all resources. Our company had to stop all production of its products that were non- essential to the war effort. The plant had to be retooled to make the carbine magazines that held the thirty caliber bullets, machine gun clips and other equipment for the armed forces. Little did I realize that someday in the future my life might depend on the very carbine magazines that I was helping to produce.

The Selective Service "Draft" Law registered all men that were of military age. All men were classified as to their physical, marital, dependency, and deferment status. Everyone received a registration number and a classification status designation. Lotteries were held each month that called up the eligible men who held the selected numbers to be drafted into service in the Armed Forces. I was registered for the draft but I received an "essential" deferment classification because I was needed to help make the tools to produce these new items for the war effort. At the end of 1943 I was notified that my deferment would be ending as the tooling was completed and the plant was now in full production of munitions.

I thought about avoiding he draft by volunteering for the Army Air Corps. I had always liked maps and thought maybe I could become a navigator. About this time the Army Specialized Training Program (ASTP) and the similar Navy V-12 programs were announced. Candidates who could meet the IQ and college entrance test score criteria would be accepted. Based on the experiences of World War I, the government decided that it was going to need medical and engineering skills after the war to rebuild the war-damaged economies of the war-torn countries and care for the casualties. Because of draft, most of the young men who would normally be receiving these skills were no longer in college. If all these men continued to be drafted into the regular Army or Navy, these skills would not be available after the war ended. So the qualified students selected were inducted into the Army or Navy and after receiving their basic military training they were assigned to a college to acquire a degree in these fields.

I took the test at the Torrington High School and I was notified that I was accepted and would be notified when to report for induction into the Army. Mr. Hughes, an old Navy vet, was the high school principal and was also the room monitor for the test. After I completed the test and remembering me as a student he asked why I wasn't applying for the Navy program. I told him that would have been my preference but I had turned twenty-one and the Navy requirement differed from the Army in that you could not have passed your twenty-first birthday.

While I was working at the Union Hardware, little did I know that the best thing in my life was about to happen. Lil came into my life! We were classmates in high school but we never really knew each other. We were in different classes following different courses so we had little contact with each other. It wasn't until later when we met again at the Union Hardware Company that I finally woke up as I found her. I fell deeply in love with her! She made heads turn and I felt I was pretty lucky to find her as I found her thoughts, likes, values and goals matched mine. We even sang some good harmony together as we drove along in my Chevy going out on dates. For the two years before I reported for duty we became very close but we had to wait until I came back before even thinking of getting married. She wrote to me every day and the mailman soon got to know my letters. It was her last letter that I received while in England that I carried with me in battle and as a POW that helped to keep me sane. I had somebody to come home to!

Lillian Yurco—My Dream Girl

Home Front

While a large portion of these memoirs has to do with my experiences surrounding the Army, we must remember what our non-combatants had to contend with during the war years. First it must be remembered that everyone was in the war effort. It was a total mobilization of all our resources, material and people. Everyone was encouraged to buy war bonds and had to sacrifice most of the comforts of life that we had become accustomed to. Practically all civilian goods were no longer manufactured or available. People were asked to turn in pots, pans and other items that were not needed for recycling into needed materials for the war.

Women had to find substitutes for nylon stockings; nylon was needed for parachutes. Gasoline rationing was in effect; gas was needed to power the vehicles of war. All new automobile production was stopped. The factories were now building tanks, jeeps, and airplanes. People did a lot more walking. Even their meals were not the same; meats like beef and ham and staples like butter and sugar were in short supply, as these were being sent to feed the armed forces. Women were called to work in the factories to fill the spots left vacant by men going into the service. Seven day and sixty hour work weeks were the minimum.

People suddenly had a lot of money after years of depression, but the irony was they still could not buy the items they may have dreamed about.

After the Pearl Harbor surprise attack there was the fear that our mainland might come under attack from the air. Again the civilian population was organized into the Civilian Defense Corps. This may also have been a morale builder for those at home as it made them feel they too were doing their share to help the War effort. Lillian was an Air Raid Warden in her neighborhood. Bombers at this time did not have radar to guide them to their targets. Bombers depended on bomb sights aimed at visual targets. At night, it would be the lights of the city. So blackouts were made when the Air Raid signals were turned on. People were instructed to cover their windows with heavy curtains and shades to prevent any light from escaping to the outside which was to be in total darkness. The Air Raid

Wardens would patrol the streets in their neighborhood to see that all citizens were complying with the instructions.

The Wardens would also receive instructions on what to do in various types of emergencies including assisting in putting out small fires. For years we had a portable water tank with a hand pump that was similar to the ones used to put out forest fires. That was the one that was stored at Lil's house when she was a warden.

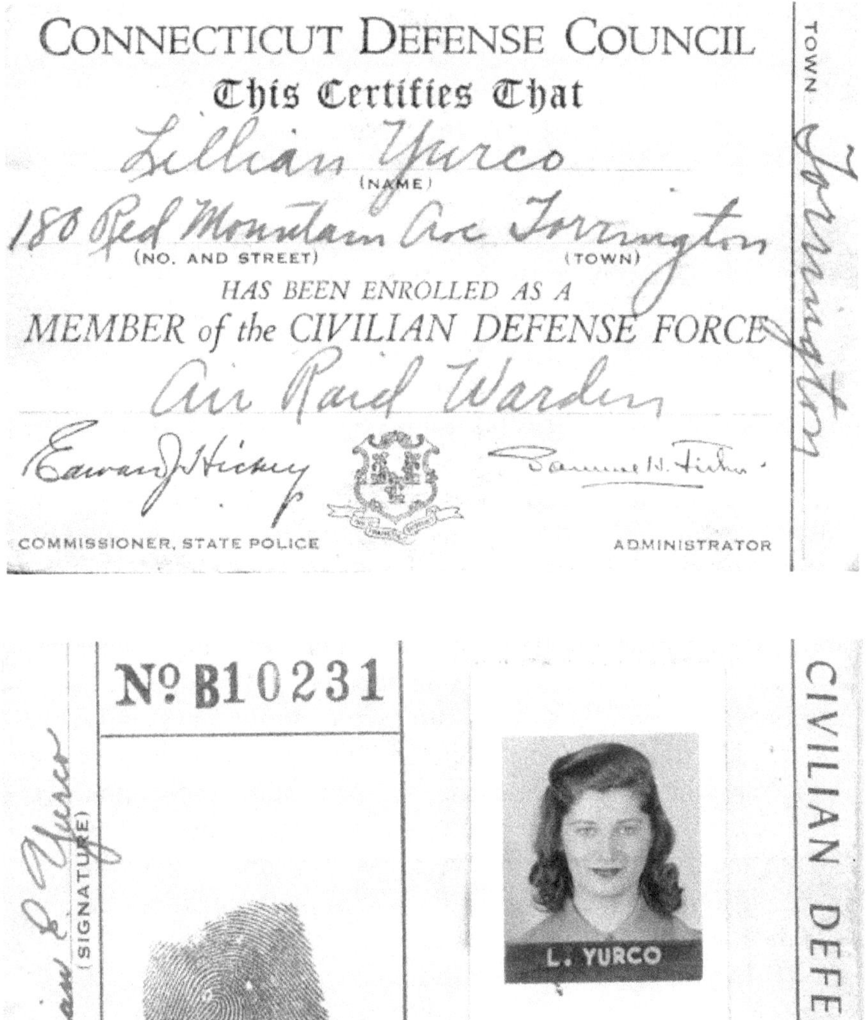

CONNECTICUT DEFENSE COUNCIL

This Certifies That

Lillian Yurco
(NAME)

180 Red Mountain Ave Torrington
(NO. AND STREET) (TOWN)

HAS BEEN ENROLLED AS A

MEMBER of the CIVILIAN DEFENSE FORCE

Air Raid Warden

Edward J. Hickey
COMMISSIONER, STATE POLICE

ADMINISTRATOR

TOWN Torrington

No B10231

Lillian E. Yurco
(SIGNATURE)

(LEFT THUMBPRINT)

L. YURCO
(PHOTOGRAPH)

CIVILIAN DEFENSE

On My Way

In June of 1943 I received orders to report to the Torrington City Hall, where we boarded a bus for Hartford, Connecticut. There we took a train to Fort Devens, Massachusetts, headquarters of the Army 1st Service Command. We stayed there a week as other ASTP candidates arrived from all over New England. Our orientation and training began along with receiving our uniforms and the packing all our civilian clothes that were sent home. Everything was GI, "General Issue," right down to the underwear and socks. Then came the physical examinations and the start of Army basic training.

It was there that I learned my first important lesson, "YOU NEVER VOLUNTEER." We arrived on Monday and we were told in the orientation that we would be chosen for various details during the week. We also were told that we could get a weekend pass provided we were not chosen for a detail on those weekend days. So I volunteered the next day for KP, the next day for another detail, and so on, so that by Friday I had served on each of the details. I could picture being home with Lil again even if it was only for few hours. I could not think of a reason that would hold me back from my pass. Wrong! Each morning after roll call, the list of those persons who were shipping out that day was read. It was Saturday morning and guess who was shipping out? Yes, an angry disappointed sad sack who felt he had been had!

We boarded a troop train in the afternoon and we were on board for several days. Our train apparently did not have a high priority for we did not take a direct route to the camp and we were side-tracked often to let other trains pass us by. We were not told where we were going, so speculation and rumors were the rule of the day. First we went west and through New York State and the next morning we stopped in some small village. Seeing some young boys by the side of the train we called out to them asking, "Where are we?"

They all replied, "uh-Hi-Ya."

We answered "Hi" and asked again and each time we received the same reply. After muttering among ourselves at what a dumb bunch they were, we finally got the message—it was Ohio. It was our first experience with a different dialect. Later in the day we found we were heading south heading toward Georgia. The next morning we were in Alabama and later that day we got off the train in Fort McClellan, near Anniston, Alabama. The training cadre who were waiting to march us to our barracks couldn't believe that we were in the Army less than two weeks. We looked like we had been through a battle. Our clothes were blackened from the soot of the steam engines and we all needed showers. The cars that were put on in Fort Devens were the old wooden Boston & Maine cars with wicker seats and single sash windows that could be opened. We speculated that the last time these cars were used must have been during World War I. (That would have been only about twenty-five years earlier.)

Now we were to receive our Infantry Basic Training. It was the same three month course used for replacements to the regular Army units. In our case we were going to go to college in September instead. That fact was not lost on the cadre of the camp. We were to pay an extra price for our good fortune. We had a first Sergeant from New Jersey that spoke in a language new to us. "You guys, ya tink yer so smart cause yer goin ta collige, wall let me tal ya som ting, yer stupid dumb blank, blank, etc. Ya put ice crem boxes in da commodes, ya"—and so on. One of his routines that he enjoyed doing was to see how fast we could change our clothes. We would "fall in" (assemble) for roll call and he would then say "I don't like your uniforms. Fall out and change into fatigues and be out here in five minutes."

We would change and run out while he was still blowing his whistle, buttoning on the way. He would always be able to find something amiss as he inspected our attire. If one person had a button undone, we all had to go back for another change. This could go on for four or five changes. If we still could not pass 100% inspection he would have us run a few miles for punishment. Of course all this was done with the usual chatter about our stupidity.

Fort McClellan was not the place to be in the summer. The red clay fits the hell hole that it was. To simulate battle conditions a field was covered with barb wire and a machine gun was placed to fire its rounds over the wire. Water was spread over the clay to make it more challenging and "bombs" of exploding black powder were placed in spots along the way. Every soldier crawled under this wire with his full battle gear. When he came out on the other end, covered with that sticky red mud, he had to fire his rifle at a target. If any mud got into the rifle barrel he had to go back and do it over again.

One very hot, humid, Alabama summer day we were wakened at 4:00 a.m. and told we were going on a forced march. After breakfast and dressed in full battle gear with full back packs we stood in formation and we were addressed by the camp commander. He read from a letter he had received from his son who was in North Africa fighting in the desert. He talked about conditions there and the lack of water. Then he told us we must learn to discipline ourselves and we were going to start today to learn how to go without water. He then ordered all canteens to be emptied. We were ordered to open ranks (increase the spaces between persons in front and back of you), open the caps of our canteens and turn them upside down to empty them. We held them in front of us while the officers walked though to insure everyone had complied with the order. Then the march began. It went on for six hours, with the usual ten minute break per hour. The Alabama sun drove the temperature up into the high nineties in the morning. About half way through the march, the men stated to drop by the side of the road and were picked up by the ambulances and trucks following the columns of men. Heat exhaustion and sun stroke was the problem. Yet the columns marched on with the numbers dwindling at an increasing rate. I managed to finish with less than half of those who started and I felt sick. The rest of the day's training schedule was canceled. Our reaction? We wondered where they managed to find such a large number of idiots to come to such a hell hole like this to train us.

ASTP

September came and now thankful that we had survived, we again boarded a train to go to our school. We were not told where we were going and because we were all from the New

England states we were hoping for a university in the northeast. What we got was a short ride to Auburn, Alabama. Over a thousand unhappy faces marched from the railroad station to the Auburn campus. Looking at the people and coeds along the way, we observed that they didn't seem to like these Yankees moving into the places that were occupied by their boys either. The next few weeks were ones of very cool looks and formal talk. That famed Southern hospitality was notably absent. Then things began to warm up as we got over our disappointment and they began to recognize that we were not that much different than their boys and soon friendships began to develop. Some of the fellows received letters from home that said that the schools up there were being filled with southern and western students. We decided this wasn't an accident, that this must have been planned to keep us far enough from home so we would not be able to take a long weekend pass. Since we had nowhere to go we would stay on campus and study.

Auburn was a nice small southern college town. The corner of the campus came right to the main business street. There were the barber shop, drug store, corner variety store, and the small hamburger hangout—I believe it was called the "Cub." The mascot of the college football team was and still is the tiger. I still remember a sight I never saw back home, scores of roaches running up and down the walls of the dimly lighted room of booths!

Segregation was still in effect in the South. It took a little getting used to for a boy from Connecticut. Blacks would never enter any restaurant unless they worked there and then they would use the back door. There were two sets of public rest rooms with signs that said *White* and *Colored.* When you got on bus or train, the blacks would wait until everyone else boarded then they would enter and go to the back of the bus. If there was not enough room to pass on a sidewalk without touching they would step aside and let you pass. There was a black employed to sweep the floor in the barber shop that I went to. I noticed that he never spoke unless he was spoken to first. Every time he mentioned anybody's name it was always preceded by "Mr." and he used "sir" frequently. He appeared happy as he supported stories of fishing with the barber but he never violated the respect that he was taught in dealing with whites. The Army, too, was still segregated. There were some special forces for the blacks. This did not change until after the war was over.

We moved into new buildings that were recently built to house the coeds and the girls were put into the fraternity houses that formally housed the male students. This was done so we could all be assembled in one section of the campus and organized like a military academy. There were six of us to a room sharing three bunk beds where before the room would be shared by two coeds. We each had two drawers and a third of a closet for our clothes. We were each allowed one picture on the dresser. Every item had to be folded or hung and arranged in the same uniform pattern and location. No extra items were allowed. In the morning we had to prepare the room for inspection while we were gone for our classes. Each drawer was pulled out two inches from the other to allow the inspector to view each drawer's contents for violations. Our beds were made up tight enough to bounce a coin and our tile bathroom was spotless and free from water droplet spots. The last man out of the rooms wiped the floor with a bath towel removing any foot prints on the floors. When we came back for our lunch break the first thing we did was to check the bulletin board in the hall for our inspection report. Each violation was called a gig. Going over the allowed number of gigs for the week meant no passes that weekend for the whole room. Returning to our rooms we could see the foot prints on the floor of the inspectors on our highly polished floors.

We wore our uniforms at all times, marched between classes, had mandatory study periods in the evening, and lights out after an hour of free time. The courses were selected for us and were just the essentials required to become an engineer—no electives or basket weaving for us in this school. We had a saying that if you dropped your pencil in class they would be on the next page before you retrieved it. That was almost true. It was not uncommon to cover a chapter in a day in some subjects. The plan was to have us get our Bachelors in three years. Some of my classmates who were in college before entering the program couldn't believe the pace that was being set.

We had our fun too. We often sang ditties or marching songs as we marched. One afternoon we were in a cocky mood and as we were marching into the stadium for our physical training exercises we broke into a Civil War song, "Marching through Georgia." Our instructors were members of the regular college faculty. This one happened to be a Southerner and he appeared noticeably angry. When we came to attention he started with this remark. "Well gentlemen, I see we are in high spirits today. For our first exercise you will run up the seats to the top row of this stadium then back down and up and down until I tell you to stop." We never sang that song again!

Our commander was a retired cavalry colonel and had been the head of the college ROTC program at Auburn. He was so happy to have a command again of real soldiers. He was like a grandfather to us, the opposite extreme from what we had just come from. We would have rifle practice with .22's a few times a month and he was always there in his riding boots. Rumor said he slept with his boots on because he wanted to be sure he died with them on. My mother died the last day of my final exams before Christmas vacation. I was not notified until I returned to my barracks and then I was brought to the colonel's office for the news. His staff had already contacted the Red Cross and had my travel papers, airline reservations and tickets ready for me. After I packed my bag they had a car ready and took me to the airport. I was touched with the compassion shown by him and his staff.

I passed the first semester but many of us decided that if we got our degree it wouldn't mean anything if we didn't get a full education. So many us put in a request for a transfer to the Air Corps. I thought now I'd go back to my previous plan to become a navigator. I thought the training could be useful toward an engineering degree later on. We took the IQ tests on campus and we all passed. (The requirements were about fifteen points lower than what was needed for the ASTP program that we were in.) We wondered why they bothered to have us take that test again. We passed the physicals and we were waiting for our call to report to Maxwell field after the end of the semester.

About a week after our acceptance there was a notice on the bulletin board when we returned from our classes. All transfers to the Air Corps had been canceled. The Armed Service Command had determined that with the Allies gaining superiority in the air, fewer replacements were needed, and the priorities were now shifting to the infantry. The cadets who had enrolled from our group during the last semester were also having their training suspended and were being transferred to the infantry. Within the month we received another notice that the ASTP Program was canceled and we were to be transferred to Army units of our basic training. Infantry. I can still hear the shouts, "We've been Shanghaied."

We marched from the campus to the train. This time everyone in town was out there, wishing us well, and yes, even tears were falling from some eyes. We had become a part of them. Indeed some of our men had become engaged to coeds that were now left behind. (In those days Southern girls came to college from small towns to find a husband. In some of the farming areas their families may have been the only white family in town. Segregation was still in practice in the South. Ninety percent of the coeds at Auburn majored in home economics.) We never had coeds in our classes or even in our school buildings as our courses were exclusively ours. Any contact with coeds would have to be outside of our compound. While I always enjoyed seeing a pretty face and a shapely body, I remained true to Lil, the one back home that they couldn't beat.

Pictures that I carried with me. Later, they kept me sane.

Co. 2 Section 5 Auburn A.S.T.P.

January, 1944

Sitting ;(Left to Right)
Hal Knight, Rochester,NY- Roy F Lent, NYC - Jack Klemens, Brooklyn, NY - Gene Judd, NYC - Stan Levine, Stamford, CT- Richard Wolhent, Boston, MA- Ernost Kinoy, NYC- Dave Keay, Brockton, MA
Kneeling; Walter Luwin, NYC - Carl Lei, Manchester, NH -Bob Lanton, Greenwood, SC -Thomas Keneshea, Providence, RI -Bill Irwin, Shelby, OH -Jim Lindsey, Nor. Creek, NY Bill Lawson, Hornell, NY
G.P.Kelly, Pittsfield, MA - I. H. Joesephs, -Brooklyn, NY
Third Row
Mel Kirzon, NYC, - Oliver Lothrop, Newton, MA - Gordy Little, Harrisburg, PA- Charles Kroartler, NYC - Ed Kushner, Brooklyn, NY -Stanley Lavietes, New Haven, CT- Dorsey Johnson,- Washington, PA
Al Landfield, - Newark, NY
Back Row:
Bob Lucy, Milton, MA - Robert D Loring, NYC - Erwin Kilgus, Philedelphia, PA - Paul Koy, Jr, Titusville, PA - **Russ Lang, Torrington, CT** - Summeret, Boston, MA - Jim Logan, Buffalo, NY - Isadore Kassel, Haverhill, MA - Albert Krause, Philedelphia, PA

Chapter Two

106th Infantry Division

The train ride took us to Camp Attebury, Indiana, where we were going to get division training prior to an assignment to a unit overseas. The 106th Infantry Division had just come off maneuvers in Tennessee with the highest score ever received by a Division. About 85% of the troops were sent overseas to other divisions as replacements for their casualties. After receiving new clothing we were standing outside waiting to hear our name called and our assignment to a regiment. The 423rd Infantry Regiment was filling its requirements and my name came up and was followed with "I Company." Then I heard the groans as I heard before when "I Company" was called. Later I heard why—it had the most demanding captain in the Division! Whatever anyone else was doing we had to go them one better. When the other companies marched, we would break into double time (jog). They would be resting in their barracks and we would be doing physical training or some other military exercises. We weren't happy with this but I'll admit we were in great shape.

Captain was a very tall thin man, all legs. When we were on those long marches and in a double time mode, some of the men could not keep up. He would call me out of formation and say, take his rifle, or some other gear he was carrying, and now I'd be carrying two rifles as we jogged along. I was not the only one who would receive this "honor." I think it was also his way of picking out the men who could keep up with this goal of his. Soon I was asked to temporarily take over the platoon in a drill on some afternoons. Later I was promoted to Corporal, becoming a squad leader for one of the 30 mm mortar squads. When the three months training period was up about 60% of the company was sent over seas as replacements to other divisions. I remained as part of the cadre for the next group coming in for division training. Looking back I never realized what Captain Moe was up to. Maybe there was a method to his madness. I think all that extra effort was his way of sorting out who he wanted to keep or who to trade away preparing for the day that he was going to take I Company overseas.

Posing in the doorway of our barracks at Camp Atterbury, Indiana during the early summer of 1944. From left to right: PFC. Panos, gunner; PFC. Russ Lang, gunner; Staff Sergeant Richard Peterson, Weapons Platoon leader, Corporal Broyles, mortar squad leader. Notice that gunners carried a .45 caliber pistol on their belt as they would also carry part of the mortar into combat. Squad leader carried mortar sight box, binoculars, and 30 mm carbine rifle.

Our 1st Lieutenant, John Collins, had played football at West Point. Soon we had team going and I was out there playing again. He was a great guy; he would do anything for his men; I really looked up to him. The team did not have to stand retreat because we would have started our football practice early and wouldn't be finished until the rest of the company had already finished their dinner. Mess Sergeant Shivers did not appreciate that at all, having to hold up some food for our dinner, clean up, etc. One evening when we came in he was going to give us a substitute dinner of leftovers because they had already disposed of the regular dinner. One of the non-coms went over to the officer's mess to find Lt. Collins. He came in and after a few words with the mess sergeant who said there was nothing else to be had except what he gave us, Collins went into the refrigerator room and pointed to some steaks that the sergeant had been saving for himself and said, cook these up, they'll do fine. We never had any more problems with late dinners. Sgt. Shivers was head chef at one of Chicago's large hotels. He did an excellent job preparing our company meals. That was why our battalion officers chose to eat at our officer's mess.

Sammy at Camp Atterbury

Among the new men assigned to our company was Sgt. Marvin (Sammy) Pate from Houston, Texas who was a volunteer from the Air Corps. He had been stationed in Miami, Florida during his whole time in the service, leading the cadets in physical training exercises. He was short but had muscles like I never saw before. He could do push ups as long as you wanted him to; I never saw him have to stop—he was incredible. Because of his rank he was given one of the three mortar squads in the company. After a few months, we were told that our division was no longer going to be a training division but we were going overseas to fight. Sammy was happy; this is why he had asked for a transfer to the infantry. He wanted to see action. Sammy never told me why but he may have had a premonition. Sammy decided to join a church. He became a Roman Catholic and he made out a will that he sent home from our camp in England. Sammy was not to come back.

I can't leave these memories without recalling Chief. Chief was part of my gun crew and I felt Lady Luck shone on me when I was assigned to his squad. He was a huge man, strong as an ox, and probably ten years older than the rest of us. He called us his kids. The mortar broke down into three pieces for carrying. Chief would often pick up the whole gun and carry it himself. We'd protest but he'd brush us aside and say *let's go.* If we were someplace where we might run into some rough characters it was always nice to have Chief by your side. He had never been moved out of the company. He had been promoted several times and just as many times he lost his stripes again. Chief was a full blooded Indian from Oklahoma. His problem was, like a lot of Indians, he and alcohol didn't mix well. After a few drinks he'd become a wild man and in a bar that meant fights and a lot of wrecked heads and furniture. When he was sober, as he was most of the time, he was gentle, cooperative, and had a great sense of humor. Ask him about his lost stripes and he'd laugh and say that the stripes didn't mean much to him, "cause I sure had fun cracking a few of those Marine skulls!"

Now the training took on an even more intensive mode and we again were given new equipment. We had a Mountain Division at Camp Atterbury that was also preparing to go overseas and they had just exchanged their reversible tan and white ski parkas for new ones. Our First Sergeant Mikkelsen, while with a detail that was picking up our new clothes in the warehouse, spotted the parkas that had been turned in. So he picked out enough of them for the officers and non-coms and had them packed in trunks that were addressed for our destination. When we got to England and the equipment was unpacked, we all looked pretty sharp in our parkas when we went to town! The other units let out a howl and one of their officers went to the battalion commander to complain. When he entered the room there was the colonel wearing a parka. He left without saying a word and that was the end of that. Then I knew why Mikkelsen was a First Sergeant!

We boarded trains again; this time the tracks were cleared for us all the way. We arrived in Fort Miles Standish, a P.O.E. (Port Of Embarkation) near Carver, Massachusetts the same day. We were not told where we were going, but we were happy that we were at a port of embarkation on the east coast and we were not going west to the Pacific war zone. I even had visions of getting a weekend pass to go home but that was not going to happen. Late Sunday afternoon we were on a train pulling out of camp.

We thought we might be going to Boston but after an hour of racing along we saw what appeared to be Long Island Sound. It was dark outside and we had been ordered to keep our window shades pulled down. After a few hours the train stopped, we raised the shade and I couldn't believe my eyes, we were in a lower level of Grand Central Station. That was the fastest train ride I ever experienced. The only people on the platform were railroad personnel. After about a half hour wait, we pulled down the blinds again and went through a tunnel to New Jersey coming to a stop at the United Fruit docks. We boarded ferry boats that took us back across the Hudson to the Cunard pier in Manhattan. As we waited in lines for the huge doors to slide open we were served coffee and doughnuts by the Red Cross.

Then the moment came as the huge doors opened and we began to move onto the ship. As we crossed the gang plank, I looked down to the water and then up to the deck. It was a long distance in both directions and we knew then this had to be one of the Queens. We were led to our stateroom and while we were lying in our bunks and talking, a British steward appeared at the door and asked if everything was all right. One of the fellows asked him, "Say, what's the name of this old tub?"

His face became flushed and with anger in his Cockney voice he said, "A tub is she, I'll ave you know she's a queen, the Queen of em all!" and he stormed out of the door. Then we knew we were on the Queen Elizabeth, the biggest and fastest liner in the world!

The ship had been stripped of her normal furnishings. Our room that would have been for two passengers now had twelve GI's. Two triple bunks on each side of the room. We had to take turns getting dressed, as there wasn't room for all of us to stand up at the same time. We were lucky; in the warmer months she would carry additional men on the open deck. Along with our whole division (14,032 men) there were many other units so I don't know how many thousand people were on board. The loading of our regiment took place most of the night and around dawn the ship slipped out of New York Harbor on October 17, 1944.

Waiting for us was our escort, U.S. Navy blimps, destroyers, etc. who were out there looking for German submarines. When it got dark they left us and we were on our own racing in a zigzag course across the Atlantic. The Queens did not travel in convoys or with naval vessels when they were on the high seas because they were too fast for the subs. They would stay out of the normal shipping lanes and keep changing course. If a sub spotted a Queen they would have to be lucky enough to be directly in front or next to it for them to be in range. The Queens were too fast for the subs to catch.

Because there were so many troops on board we had strict rules to follow on board. We were allowed a limited area to roam, as they didn't want to shift too much weight to one side to list the ship. We had two meals a day, usually greasy British foods like mutton, salt pork, and Valencia oranges that were the size of a large lemon. We also had exercise sessions and life boat and evacuation drills. On our last day at sea as we were approaching Scotland, large British Flying Boats appeared and then soon the British and American naval ships came to escort us into the Clyde River. Later we arrived in the port for

Glasgow, Scotland on October 22nd. This was the deep water port where the Queens were built.

It was a beautiful fjord surrounded by high mountains that came right down to the water. Trains traveling along the water's edge would disappear and reappear several times as they passed through tunnels. Looking through binoculars at the tops of those mountains, we saw they were covered with anti aircraft guns. The harbor almost looked like an airfield, with several aircraft carriers at anchor. The port was never bombed during the war, and if you saw it you would understand why. Even with all that ordinance it did not spoil the natural beauty of Greenock.

As we disembarked we were given refreshments by the Scots and a band was playing. We boarded trains and after passing through many tunnels we climbed out of Greenock and were on our way through the lovely country side of Britain. We arrived in the rolling country side of the Midlands and soon, passing many thatched-roofed cottages, we came to our next home, the converted stables at the famous horse racing track at Cheltenham, England. Here we would spend the month of November waiting for our supplies and equipment to arrive and then to check it out. Each day we hiked and trained to sharpen our skills. We bought a few used bikes and rode around the countryside during our time off.

I went to London for a few days with a few of my buddies. We stayed in some rooms in a building across from a park. One evening we were across town when we were caught in an air raid. The sirens went off and we ran following others down into a shelter. After the all clear we came out and found that the area where we were escaped damage. When we got back to our building later that night we learned that there was now a crater in the park across the street from a V2 rocket that fell there. Not all of the rockets fell out of harm's way; we saw evidence of many hits in the city. Rationing was in effect and menus offered the minimum menus with very little sweets to offer. We liked the fish 'n chips you could buy from a stand wrapped in a newspaper. The newspaper was rolled in a cone shape and it served to absorb the cooking oil that was on the fish and potatoes.

Too soon we were ready to go—we liked England but it was back to the trains and we were on our way to Southampton. As we marched from the train station to the docks we passed a shipyard where workers were busy making parts on huge lathes and presses. What was interesting was there were no walls on the building, just a roof. They were really working outside! We boarded small Army transports and ferries and crossed the English Channel to Le Havre, France. It was December 6, 1944.

Le Havre is the seaport on the mouth of the Seine River and is the port for Paris. When the Germans retreated as the Allies landed during that spring, they blew up every building that could be of some value to the Allies. This was done in the port and both sides of the river for miles almost to Paris. The docks were all gone. The Army Engineers had constructed a temporary pier out of large pontoons that looked like tin cans tied together and covered with timber. The pier surface rolled with the wave action. As we came off the pier and were loaded on to trucks we looked around. It was unbelievable; not a building was standing, nothing but piles of rubble everywhere, and this continued until we left the river area and were into the farming countryside.

It had been a rainy day and about mid afternoon our convoy reached its destination, some farm land along a dirt road in Limésy, France. This was our camp for the next three days as we waited for the rest of the units that were assigned to the division to come over from England. So into the muddy fields we went and pitched our tents. Each soldier carries one half of a pup tent in his pack, called a *shelter half.* Two men team up and button the shelter halves together to make the tent. I don't remember what we put over the mud but I think it must have been straw from the farm.

The French farmers had offered their barns but our officers would not have any of that. No sir, we wouldn't think of it, at least not for the enlisted men! Sergeant LaMontaino said he was of French descent and we were a tent team. On the ship finding out that I knew some German he told me that we should make out okay. In France he would be able to get by and when we got to Germany I would take over. On the second evening in our tent he said that he felt like getting some fresh eggs. All we got so far were the dry powdered variety that you mixed with water. He said why don't we slip out to the farm house and see if they will sell us some, or maybe we could trade with them for some chocolates or cigarettes.

So across the dark field we traveled to the large house that must have belonged to the owner. As we approached the house there was a Jeep in front of the door. Some of our officers were there. We couldn't go in there—we weren't supposed to be away from camp. Then we spotted a small house down the road and as we walked to it, it looked like no one was there. We knocked at the door. Soon an old man opened it and seeing our uniforms he invited us in. Soon his wife and children came in to the parlor to see the Americans.

LaMontaino was silent after his *bon jour*, and not responding to the Frenchman's questions. I said to him, okay, do your stuff, tell him why we are here. LaMontaino then tells me he doesn't know how! Great, so pulling my little French/English dictionary from my pocket and using my "C" high school French and with hand language we began communicating. The little girl came by my side and I would point to the French word that I couldn't pronounce and she would say it then I told her the English word for it. I told them that we would like to buy or trade with them for two eggs. The man spoke to his wife too fast for me to understand and she left the room. We labored on, he asking questions and responding to ours. We determined that he was a worker on this large farm and he confirmed that the large house belonged to the owner. More than enough time went by for his wife to get the eggs and we started wondering what was taking her so long.

After a while she reappeared and she motioned to us to follow her into the kitchen. The family followed and the man then motioned for us to sit at the table that had been set for us. Soon she came with her skillet and served us two fried eggs each with a little bacon and French bread. We were overwhelmed, what hospitality! It was their way of showing their appreciation for our coming to help their country. We must have spent a few hours with them and we were about to leave when the man asked how long we were going to be there. We told him that we were leaving toward Germany the next day. He told us to wait and motioned to us to sit again and left the room. Soon he reappeared with a bottle of brandy and a framed photograph. The picture was of him when he was a soldier in World War I. He then pointed to his skull where he indicated that a bullet had grazed him. Then he poured drinks for the three of us and drank a toast for our safe return. As we left and said our good-byes we gave the children our chocolate bars. Passing the big house the Jeep was still there, but now we were happy that it was there; we would have missed a most memorable evening.

After breakfast we broke camp and soon we were back in the trucks and on our way over pitted, rough roads. We passed though interesting small towns and battered villages, past burned skeletons of tanks and trucks in the roadside ditches. Our trucks wound through the mountains of Eastern Belgium and Luxembourg passing snow covered evergreens that looked like a Christmas card. It was a beautiful scene. The area reminded me of being back in Connecticut. We passed through St. Vith, with people waving to us as we drove by and giving the Vee for Victory sign and we returned them. In a little while, we were over the German border, where we stopped.

We then marched through fog and thick snow to our positions in the area that was the called the Schnee Eifel, a wooded, snow-covered ridge overlooking the village of Sellerich. It was late in the afternoon of the 11th of December. The veteran 2nd Infantry Division, whom we were relieving, passed us heading back for the trucks that were taking them to a rest area in the rear. Then they were going join in a planned attack to capture the Roer River dams to the North. It was believed that these dams could be opened by the Germans to flood the area that would be in the path of an Allied offensive, so their capture was a high priority.

Infantry on the march, December 1944.

Front line in Western Europe prior to Battle of the Bulge. Author's unit occupied Schnee Eifel.

When planning offensives, part of the strategy is to overpower the opponent with as much force as one can muster. The Allied troops were covering a long front from Holland to the Swiss border. Our Division was the last division to leave the USA; there were no more divisions left. With such a long front there just were not enough reserves to provide the power needed to mass for an offensive and still be able to maintain a normal distribution of manpower to safely hold the occupied positions in the line. So troops had to be taken out of the line to mass an offensive. Our division was to occupy a "*quiet*" area, an area that was some twenty-two miles long that should have been a five mile front under normal conditions. The 2nd Division had requested that part of the line that formed a salient into Germany be pulled back to shorten the line, to make it more easily defendable and reduce the exposure to encirclement.

Our high command refused the request because it did not want to give up its salient position into the Siegfried line—a position that later could be used as a jumping off point for a future offensive to reach the Rhine River. In addition, our Army high command was sure that the Germans were in no position to mount an offensive of their own. There was little contact made by us with the departing 2nd Division except for a very brief meeting and tour of the front by the officers.

The following is from the story of the 106th Division.

> *This was a quiet sector along the Belgium-German frontier. For ten weeks there had been only light patrol activity and the sector was assigned to the 106th so it could get some experience. The baptism of fire that was to come was the first action for the 106th. For many of its men it was the last. The little road center of St. Vith had seen war before. It was through St. Vith that Nazi panzers rolled to Sedan in 1940; German infantry marched through it in 1914. But it never had figured as a battleground such as it was to become in this fateful December of 1944. During the night of Dec. 15, front line units noticed increased activity in the German positions.*

Actually our riflemen were calling back on their phones to the command post on December 13th and 14th. On the 15th the reports that were coming from our forward posts said the noises sounded like tanks out there. The command post relayed all the messages up to Battalion and it went on up through Division HQ in St. Vith. The answer that came back on all the nights including the 15th was that your men are hearing things, it's your imagination. They wrote us off as green inexperienced troops with the jitters. Later I read that one of the answers that we received was, "They are playing records to scare you!" That says a lot about our "intelligence staff" that were back in France.

My mortar squad was located along side of a dirt road in a dug-out hole that was built up and covered with large logs and dirt. There was an opening facing the road for our mortars so we could shoot over the trees on the other side. Our position was the last one for our company along the dirt logging road. We were near a pill box that was part of the West Wall or what the Germans called the Siegfried Line. We took turns manning that post day and night. A patrol would walk the road every few hours to make contact with the next unit that was a considerable distance away. Some of these gaps in the line were a few miles across. You could move a company of men through one and nobody would ever hear them. German patrols would be out there often. One night one of their police dogs broke away and was chasing something down the road. The dog was shot as it ran past our position.

In the early morning hours of December 16th all hell broke loose. We were under very intense artillery and rocket fire. We hugged the ground in our log shelters for what seemed an eternity (probably about a half hour) but even with the tree bursts my squad made it through OK without any casualties. As the morning progressed we could hear occasional shooting and shelling to our front and flanks. Slowly the firing sounds started to come around to the rear.

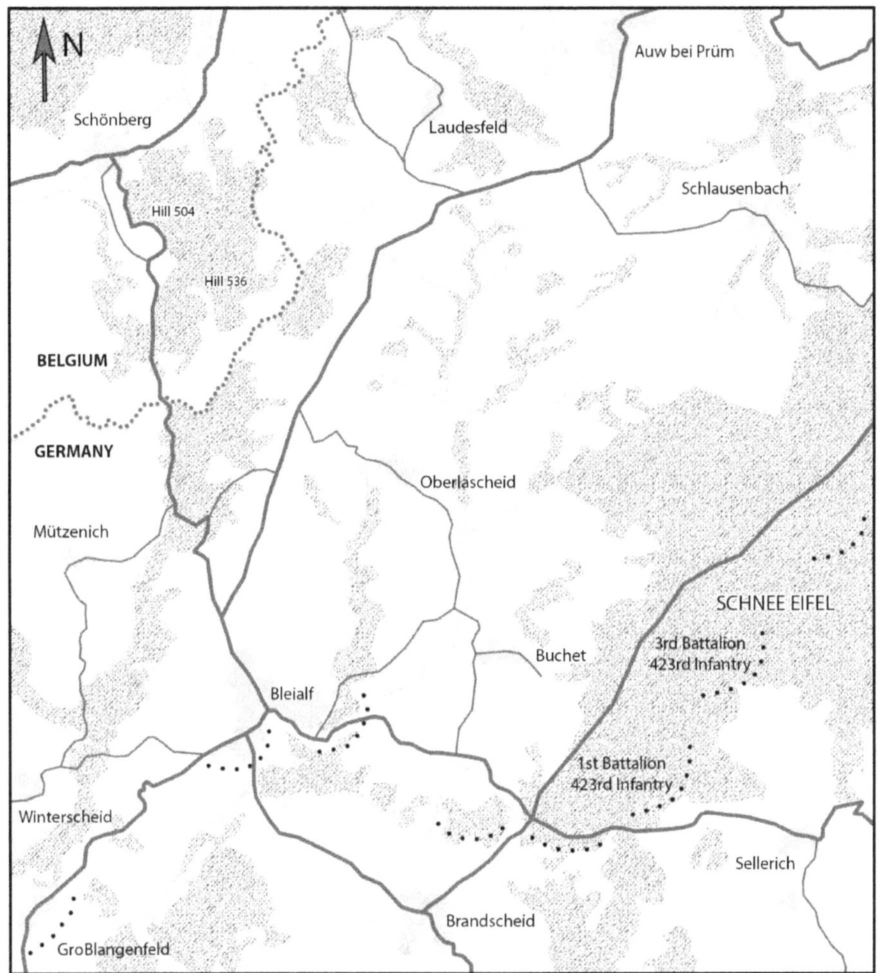

Position of author's regiment (423rd) December 16, 1944

The heavy artillery blasting cut the telephone lines to our front so we didn't know what was going on and we had no requests for mortar fire. In the late afternoon some of our rifle platoons appeared coming out of the woods and going to our rear. When asked where they were going we were told they were going to set up positions in the rear. Soon we received orders to move some of our mortar to the opposite side of the road facing the rear and to prepare the site for firing. We knew then that we were surrounded. No attack came that night although we could hear gunfire in the distance to the rear of our position.

The next morning, on the 17th of December, we were told that we were going to break out of our encirclement. We were told to destroy anything that could not be carried forward into the attack. Blankets, overcoats, excess ammo, etc., were burned or blown up. Rumor was that we were headed toward St. Vith and we would draw new supplies there. Our company commander was notorious for not passing information down to his men. Most of the time we didn't know where we were going, we were just told to keep going down the road or path we were on. (A few light tanks or armored vehicles I believe that were from the 9th Armored came into position on the road.) With Jeeps and our trucks ready to follow, we started to march out in columns. Ahead of us were the rifle platoons leading the assault. Occasionally we would stop as we heard shooting ahead of us but we received no calls for support and we soon would resume our advance. Around noon we passed a German field kitchen, its pots were boiling over, raising columns of steam as the contents spilled into the fire as they were left in haste by the retreating German troops. We were surprised and felt elated at what seemed to be shaping up as such an easy victory! Practically no resistance; we did not know that the main enemy forces had decided to bypass us and had headed on toward Schönberg and St. Vith.

In mid-afternoon we were approaching a town. It may have been Radscheid about one and a half miles from Schönberg. The road we were following curved up Hill 536. It was a high hill with open fields on each side and woods to their rear. As we approached the crown of the hill the sky opened up and we were the targets of a vicious artillery and anti aircraft batteries of fire that rained down a tremendous bombardment that seemed endless. In a few minutes everything on the road was destroyed. We had dived into whatever ditch or cover that we could find along the side of the road. As the shells continued to explode around us I was very frightened. How could I survive out in this open space? Surely a piece would find me in this shallow ditch. When the fire finally lifted we ran into the woods to regroup and take up defensive positions. This may have been the artillery battalion that was moved out of Schönberg to join into the German counterattack. In the Army's history of the battle, it was mentioned there were heavy traffic jams in Schönberg due the large number of armor and panzer units moving through the town. Therefore only one German battalion was able to get into position to hit our road. Well, that was all they needed, because we didn't have a single vehicle left.

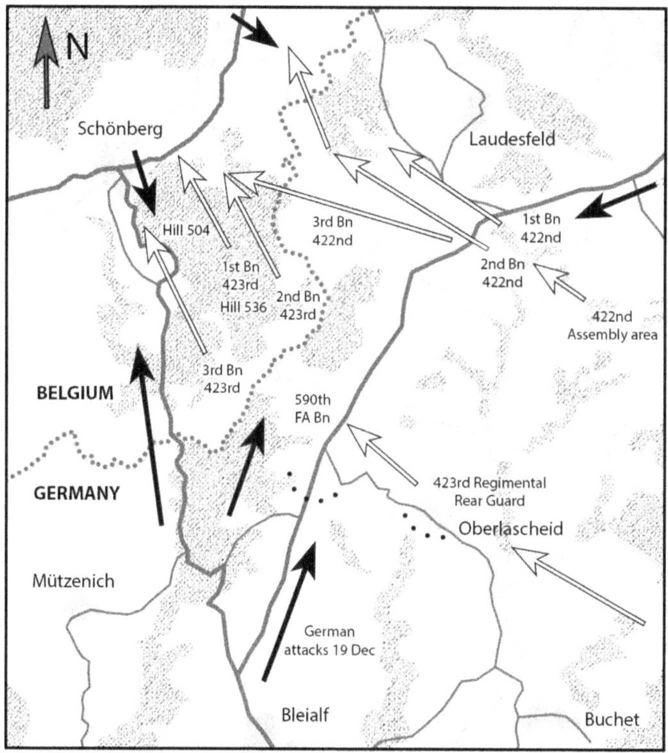

Positions on December 19, 1944

All we had was what we were carrying on our backs. We reassembled in the woods to the side of the road and continued our advance toward Schönberg. We were on Hill 536 where we ate our K rations and drank water from our canteens and we stopped for the night.

The next morning (December 18th) we refilled our canteens with water taken from a brook and put in purification tablets. (I believe they contained an iodine compound.) We continued on our advance to the next hill, 504. (I had no idea what hill number we were going to at the time; the only command we got was "let's go," and we followed the others.) We could hear the rifle fire of the rifle platoons ahead of us but they were not in need of much mortar support. We occupied Hill 504 that was our objective outside of Schönberg. We were wondering if we were going to get a re-supply of food and munitions. Maybe we would get the 424th Infantry reserves or 7th armor support from St. Vith to help us. Nothing came; we were on our own on this advance. We spent another night hungry and freezing in the woods but the Germans left us alone. (Actually, transport planes had left England with the supplies we needed that were going to be air dropped, but due to a foul up in communications in the Air Force command, they had to be diverted to France. The 7th Armor had been ordered to come to our support but turned back a few miles from reaching us. They decided they did not want to risk the loss of tanks and fell back to stronger positions in the new line being formed with the 424th Regiment.)

The morning of the 19th found us advancing again in another attempt to reach Schönberg only to withdraw and then move on to try again in another location. About mid afternoon my squad and another under Sammy Pate were called upon to lay down some mortar fire for our rifle platoons that were ahead of us. There was a small clearing in the woods that would allow us to set up the mortars. I ran out into the field and I dropped the gun-sight box at the location where I wanted my crew to set up the gun. Then I continued to run ahead to take up a position to observe and to direct the mortar fire. (At this point I had no idea what I was going to be looking for! As usual there was no information from our officers, just to get out there. I was hoping I would see the target as I got to the end of the field. Anyway Sammy would be out there with me I thought and we would find it. I think somebody might have said it was a German 88 artillery piece.) While running to about the middle of the clearing, with my binoculars now pulled out from my jacket and hanging from my neck, I came under sniper fire from the left side of the field.

I dove for the ground. Each time I raised my head attempting to see where the fire was coming from, the sniper would fire at me, the bullets whistling by my helmet. When the sniper wasn't firing at me he was firing to my rear, at Sammy I thought. I had assumed that Sammy was behind me and I thought that he was doing the same thing that I was doing. I don't know how long I was out there, but it seemed like a very long time. Someone from the rear yelled not to move and to keep my head down. Finally I heard a small explosion that came from the direction of where the sniper was and then a call came from the rear to crawl back. The sniper had been killed. I began to crawl back through the snow to the cover of the woods when I noticed that Sammy was not moving, he was lying perfectly still. As I drew next to him my worst fears were confirmed, he had been shot right between the eyes, the sniper's aim was flawless. Sammy was white and there was nothing that could be done. He was dead.

As I came back and reported Sammy's death, a deep sense of guilt came over me for still being alive. It could have just as easily been me. We were both out there alone, I thought, looking up, trying to spot where the fire was coming from, but for Sammy the bullet found its mark. I remember asking under my breath, *Why not me, Lord? Why Sammy?* This was a ghost that was to haunt me for over fifty years.

For years as I remembered Sammy, I felt that I should tell his family what happened. All I knew about him was his name and that he came from Texas. That wasn't much to go on. One evening in late January 2000, I was reading an e-mail note from John Kline, editor of the 106th Infantry Division Association "Cub" magazine. He was describing finding the grave of one of our regiment's soldiers in Belgium. I wondered if John could check out that cemetery to see if Sammy was there. I asked him if he could find any information with his knowledge and access of the military archives. He checked out the cemeteries but did not find him. He said it was possible that his family had his body returned to the USA.

John then gave me the addresses of some the members of my unit, Company I. This turned out to be a gold mine source of information. He connected me with Richard Peterson, my mortar section leader, and other members of Sammy's mortar squad. A continual flow of Internet, mail, and phone massages with new information followed and later reunions with the men of my section. Two of Sammy's crew, Harold (Sparkie) Songer and Murray Stein were able to tell me of what really happened in that field that afternoon

The following is what Sparkie told me.

> *When the sniper started shooting, Colonel Cavender our Regimental commander was in our area and he spotted the sniper location. None of the crews had left the woods yet and Sammy was close by. He told Sammy and our crew to "Get that God damn sniper that is in those bushes over there." Sammy and his crew moved out into the clearing to set up the mortar. The range was too short to use the standard elevating mechanism. Sammy, my squad leader was trying to aim the mortar tube by elevating the tube by holding it vertically with the bottom resting on the ground. It was while he was doing this that he was killed by a bullet that hit him in the temple. At the same time, I was hit but the bullet lodged in my mess kit spoon that was in my shirt pocket. Then another mortar man (Stein) and I grabbed the mortar and dropped three shells in the area of the sniper, killing him.*

The sniper firing that I heard was not just at Sammy and me but at Sammy, his gun crew and me!

When Sammy was in England, he was a roommate of Sgt. Richard Peterson. He decided to write his will. He had Dick witness it, so Dick signed it and then put his home address on it and Sammy sent it home. Later after Sammy's parents received the news of his death they found Richard's address on Sammy's will and they contacted his parents. After Richard came home he wrote to Sammy's sister. In the 1950's Harold Songer, who was with him when he was shot, visited Sammy's mother, family and girlfriend in Houston and told them how Sammy had died.

It was in February 2000 when I first knew of what really happened. I felt a load come off of me and the ghost was gone as I knew someone had contacted the family. The blast that I heard before I crawled back was from Sammy's crew. By the time I received the call to return and then when I started to go back, they were all out of the field and back in the woods, except for Sammy. Now I know not only what happened that afternoon but who it was that may have saved my life.

Shortly after coming back from the field there wasn't time to discuss what happened as we were now on the move again. Although I didn't know it then, we were not retreating or trying to escape the Germans but we were advancing in preparation of an attack on the town of Schönberg. As I said before, our captain told us nothing of what was going on.

Soon we were nearing Schönberg. Company K and our Company I were coming down the side of Hill 504 approaching the outskirts of Schönberg when we were counterattacked by a German force coming at us through the woods from our side. S/Sgt. Richard Peterson, our mortar section leader, took one of the mortar tubes and elevating it without the mechanism, found an opening in the trees and fired off all the rest of the mortar shells we had left. There was a tremendous series of tree bursts over the advancing German rifle men forcing them to fall back in retreat. We then were preparing to spend the night after reporting our losses and ammo status and there was a lull in the fighting.

All was quiet about four-thirty that afternoon when the non-coms were called to our company captain's command post for orders. It was then that we were told that our Regimental Commander, Colonel Cavender, had issued an order to prepare for surrender in a half hour. We could not believe our ears and we asked that the order be repeated. After giving instruction of how to destroy our arms and equipment, we were told where to assemble to wait for the Germans to capture us. This came as a complete surprise and shock. I knew that we had not had anything to eat for a few days and we had no mortar rounds left. Maybe I still expected that help would still be coming from somewhere. Strangely, it never occurred to me that we would be surrendering in regimental force.

We went back to our squads and after spreading the word we began to destroy all arms and equipment that might fall into enemy hands. We took a small pick and dented the mortar barrel, destroyed the sight, removed the trigger assemblies from the rifles, carbines and pistols and after pulling the retaining pins we scattered the parts of our weapons in the snow. We buried of what we had left of the small arms ammunition in the snow. A tear came to my eye as I poked out the lens of my binoculars with the pick. I had thought that I would be bringing them home with me after the war was over. After we completed the destruction of all useful weapons and equipment, we went to the designated assembly area and waited with the others for where the surrender was to take place.

Now we were assembled in a clearing without our weapons and with all our officers, standing in front of us, waiting for the Germans to arrive.

Sammy

Sammy once again came to mind. Again I relived that last action. I thought about him lying out there on that cold snow. That was only a few hours ago. It seemed all so useless, we gained nothing, the sniper stopped us and now it's all over. Sammy should be standing with us now, I thought. Sammy's memory never left me. I knew him for such a short time, yet it seems that he became a part of me.

My remorse was suddenly interrupted with the approaching gray forms coming through the trees. They were here, their rifles pointing at us and soon they formed a ring around us. Now that they were closer they were so young looking and they looked like they were wearing Luftwaffe uniforms! First Lt. Collins, our executive officer and a few others had tried to escape the net but was quickly discovered and returned to the assembly. All of the officers were asked to step forward and after lining them up in columns they were marched away. Then the rest of us were lined up and were marched for a few hours until we came into a large field that had been quickly made into a holding pen with a barbed wire fence. I don't remember getting any food or water that night. I think we ate snow. The next morning we were led to a road and began our long march to the railroad station. We were never interrogated for they had all kinds of officers to question, from the Colonel right on down.

Our Contribution

The Battle of the Bulge was Hitler's last major attempt to split the Allied forces on the Western front in half and gain a major military victory. General von Rundstedt led fifteen German divisions against the 106th Division and the 14th Cavalry that were spread thinly along a twenty-seven mile front line. Our regiment was in the point of deepest penetration into the Siegfried Line. The German strength included some of their top Panzer and SS divisions and with this huge superiority they had expected to reach the English Channel in a few days. My mortar squad was stationed in a dug out emplacement with a heavy log and sod roof. It was on the shoulder of a dirt road in the Schnee Eifel, a wooded, snow covered ridge overlooking the village of Sellerich, Germany. The next company was about a half mile down the road to our right.

Three German armies consisting of 200,000 men attacked the front held by the 2nd, 28th, 99th, and the 106th divisions of the American 1st Army in the Schnee Eifel near the German - Belgian border. *The actions of the 422nd and 423rd in delaying the Germans for three days proved an important part of the final American victory. This gave time to build the defense of Bastogne. Their efforts were completely forgotten in the publicity given to the battles of Bastogne, which required fifteen American divisions plus support units (Air Force) to break the back of the German Army.*

Mistakes—Big Ones

The excerpts in italics are from Dr. Richard Peterson's book *Healing the Child Warrior*. These are some of the events that went wrong and that were out of control of the 106th Infantry Division but led to the demise of the 422nd and 423rd Regiments of the Division.

> *Apparently no officer was satisfied with the positions assigned to the 423rd in the Ardennes campaign.*

Most would have had the Regiments pulled out of the salient to form a straight line on the top of the ridge for a better defensive position. The Supreme Army Command still refused to give up the penetration that later became easily encircled into a trap.

> *General Robertson, commander of the 2nd Infantry Division, which we replaced in the line, advised our 106th commander, Gen. Jones, of an area of seven miles of unfortified area that provided an excellent corridor for a break through. When Gen. Jones asked Eighth Corps Commander, Troy Middleton for the return of the 2nd Battalion that was in reserve for the area, the answer was no. Then he asked where the armor was located that he could call in. Troy's answer was "There is no Armor, there is no help in case of an attack up there."*

This was exactly the area the main force of the German Panzers used in their break-through. This was also the same corridor used by the Germans in their invasion of Belgium in both World War I and World War II! Incredible !!

> *General Hodges staff discounted the reports of the German heavy armored movements made by Gen.*

Jones, commander of the 106th. He was told, "Don't be so jumpy, the Krauts are just playing phonograph records to scare you newcomers."

General Troy Middleton ordered the 7th Armored to assist the trapped regiments in breaking out of the trap. Fearing such an action would wipe out units he had in St. Vith, General Bruce Clark elected not go to the rescue of the 422 & 423 Regiments, but kept his units intact for the defense of St. Vith.

Little blame for the death of the regiments is laid on the Air Force which totally screwed up their efforts to drop desperately needed supplies. Twenty- three C-47 aircraft loaded with ammunition and medical supplies left England and arrived over a base at Florennes, Belgium, on December eighteenth. The controller waved them off because of an overload of traffic. No one informed them that the transports were on their way and were to pick up a fighter escort to take them to the drop area. The planes landed in France, but the commander still could not get any information about the regiments or their location.

These same supplies were later dropped in Bastogne for their successful and well-publicized defense. Later the Allied high command moved all supplies out of England to France to make them more accessible!

We are all human and therefore we all can and do make mistakes. My review of the above mistakes is to show that the men of the 106th faced impossible odds with little or no support. *The beleaguered regiments have never been given full credit for providing the time for those old Army units to pull back including the 2nd Division and the 9th Armored* to build new defensive lines.

The 422nd and the 423rd did not withdraw. They attacked *from the beginning of the battle until the decision to stop the slaughter was made. Only we who saw the pain in Cavender's eyes on Hill 504 at 1500 on December 19, 1944, as he assessed the*

> *impossible situation, hold an indication of his agony. Middleton and others must accept the responsibility for the terrible losses of material and men.*

Cover up?

> *Copies of memoranda in the Army Historical Library confirm that no military commander willingly exposes his mistakes in judgment. In response to suggestions to commemorate the anniversary of the Battle of the Bulge, General Eisenhower, Chief of Staff, on December 18, 1945 wrote to Robert Patterson, then Secretary of War. "I am unalterably opposed to making public at this time any story concerning the Ardennes Battle or even of the allowing any written explanation to go outside of the War Department. I thoroughly believe we should . . . say nothing whatsoever to anyone except in response to casual inquiry from our friends."*
>
> *To his credit Patterson responded to Eisenhower on December 19, 1945: "I believe the main features of this operation (Ardennes Battle) - the events leading up to it, the incidents of the fighting and the outcome -* ***should be made known to the American people****. Otherwise they will hear nothing but fault finding and many of them will think* ***the Army is covering up."***
>
> *The sanguine attitude toward any discussion of the largest land battle in the history by the former Commander of SHAEF is astonishing. In spite of Eisenhower's desire to limit discussions to "casual inquiries from our friends," the confusing story continued to unfold.*

I have heard that many of the combat veterans of these regiments have carried a guilt complex all of their lives needlessly because of this cover-up. I have talked to some of them. Dr. Richard Peterson in writing his book *Healing the Child Warrior* is to be commended for his research in his attempt to rectify the wrong that was allowed to rest on the shoulders of these men.

60 mm Mortar

The 60 mm mortar was the weapon used by the three mortar squads in a rifle company. It has the capability to fire mortar shells that explode into deadly shrapnel when the shell makes contact with an object. It can also deliver smoke shells to lay down a smoke screen cover for the protection of the rifle platoons. The squad leader runs out into a clearing to mark the spot where the mortar is to be set up. He drops the gun sight box at that point. He then continues forward to a spot where he can observe the target and direct the fire of the gun crew. He gives the range, traverse direction, and number of rounds to be fired. Upon seeing the gun sight dropped the crew goes to the spot and sets up the mortar. There is a heavy base plate that the tube fits into, two legs to stabilize the tube and the gun sight that are attached.

In the field the sight was aimed by the squad leader. In a prepared position, aiming stakes would have been put in the ground for specific target locations. Care had to taken to be sure there were no tree branches, or other objects that would contact the sensitive fuse. The shell has a spring loaded safety pin near the nose that is locked in place with a wire. This allows handling of the shell without exploding it as long as the wire is locked in place. As soon as the wire is removed and the pin is ejected by the spring, the shell is armed and will go off on contact. In the picture you will see the gunner holding his thumb over the pin in the shell, the wire has been removed, and as he drops the shell into the tube, the pin is still in place. The back end of the shell has a shot gun shell in place that hits a firing pin in the bottom of the tube. This causes the shell to be fired and propels the shell out of the tube toward its target. The pin is ejected as the shell leaves the tube, arming it. Distances can be increased by adding small bags of powder to the back of the shell before it is dropped into the tube.

Chapter Three

My POW Diary

The following is from the original penciled log book written by me, Russ Lang while a Prisoner Of War in Germany during World War II. Additional detail and comments were added from memory and are enclosed in parentheses.

> Friday February 16, 1945
> Today marks the 60th day as a POW. When thinking back of all that has happened since my capture, I find some of the details are slipping away from me. In order that I should not forget these lessons learned the hard way, I'm going to keep this log book. I'm going to use Bob Wood's diary to highlight some of the things that happened these past two months.
>
> I was captured December 19, 1944 near the St. Vith sector of the West Wall (Siegfried line). We were all hungry and except for a couple of D-bars (chocolate) and K rations I had nothing to eat since the attack started three days earlier. The Luftwaffe guards took us to a barbed wire enclosure and threw us turnips that were growing in a nearby field. The next day we were marched behind the German lines for several hours to a barnyard some miles away. On the route we passed a long line of German tanks and equipment moving into the attack.
>
> It surprised me to see the large amount of horses in use and delighted me to see the number of motor vehicles stalled on the highway. We had no place to sleep in the barnyard as it was muddy as a pig pen. On the morning of December 21 we got some water to drink and again we moved down the road. We passed a sight I could never forget—wrecked American Jeeps with dead Americans lying nearby—two of them Medics, all of them were stripped of their shoes and socks and just left lying there. I thought of Lil's cousin Jack for the Jeep was a 592nd Field Artillery vehicle. I hope he made it all right.

German tank; American prisoners

On the road there were all kinds of litter for we were tearing up all papers that we didn't reach during our surrender. As far as you could see there was the long line of prisoners and it made you feel so small and insignificant. Whenever we stopped we'd try to find some raw vegetables that may have been overlooked in the fields. We continued our walk all that day and half of the night, the Jerry telling us only a few more kilometers and then they would give us rations. We passed through more of the West Wall defenses and several towns and villages. The guards told the people they had all of Eisenhower's Army there—it must have been a good morale builder at that. We finally stopped at a huge hotel on the 22nd but we had to stay penned up in the yard with no place to sleep. The building was full with wounded and the yard was overcrowded with us. LaMontaino, Broyles and I tried to sleep in a doorway but a guard chased us away. I managed to find a seat in a barn window sill and I shivered there the last few hours of dawn.

They lined us up again that morning of December 23rd and gave us one can of limburger cheese for seven men and two bags of hard biscuits apiece. We ate for the first time. It was good. We then marched down to the railroad station in Gerolstein and we were loaded onto box cars. They had livestock in them before we got on for the manure was still on the floors. We covered it the best we could with straw but some of it still got on our clothes. Sixty-four men were crowded into a car, and there we stayed for seven days and six nights from December 23rd through December 29th.

We could not stretch out; there was not enough room. Some stood up, some sat with three sets of legs layered on top of each other. Because of the winter the moisture from our breath froze on the walls making it a sheet of ice. People in the center of the car were perspiring from the body heat of bodies tightly packed. Those on the perimeter of the car were freezing next to the iced walls. About every hour the person(s) on the bottom of the pack would scream out begging to be let up as they could not move or bear the weight of the legs on top of them. Then everyone would get up move to a new position. The ones from the outside to the center to warm up and the ones from the center to the outside to cool off—and so it went throughout the day and night.

Some of those nights I thought I'd go mad! We would urinate and pass waste into some of our steel helmets that were emptied when the doors were opened. Then we were given water to drink using other steel helmets. All of our equipment, overcoats, and blankets were left back in the battle zone. I started to make a spoon out of wood and saved an empty cheese can for a dish. On the whole trip we got a half a loaf of bread with sorghum molasses three times and barley soup once. We stayed on the train in the Limburg rail yards the last three days.

This is how we spent the 1944 Christmas. We sang carols, and prayed on Christmas Eve as one POW read from his New Testament. Another POW, a Chaplain was allowed to come to each car earlier, the door was opened by guards and he was allowed to lead us in prayer and a five minute service. Home, and the lives we lived before certainly seemed more like paradise to all of us. Christmas Eve was not to remain peaceful very long. That night the British came to bomb Limburg. We heard the sirens and we could see the guards running for the shelters dug into the side of the hill next to the tracks. One of our POWs had managed to hide a cutting pliers and he cut away the wires that covered the small open window in the corner of the car. We pushed him out the window, then he cut the wires locking our doors and the doors of several cars until the first wave of planes roared overhead. We left our car and headed for the hills on each side of the tracks. We thought the planes were going to bomb the trains but we believe the target was an oil refinery on the other side of the hill.

Some of the bombs fell short and hit the hill with the shelter. Some of our POWs died with some of the Germans in the shelter. Eddie and I were lying on the opposite bank when the bombs fell. We were hit with rocks and dirt but unhurt. We got up and ran over the top of the hill into a meadow and stayed there until the raid was over. Then we kept going with others who had escaped the cars but we were soon met by a ring of soldiers who brought us back to our cattle car. The next morning a German officer scolded us for trying to escape. He said the train was clearly marked with red crosses on the roofs and we would have been safe if we had stayed put. We were skeptical because we had heard that the Nazis had marked other trains carrying their troops with red crosses. There was a memorial service that Christmas morning in the rail yard for those POWs and Germans who died. We watched from our opened door.

When we arrived at Stalag XIIA near Limburg we were some sad sights, dirty, smelling, with over ten days of beard growth on our faces. We learned that an officers' barracks had been hit during that night's air raid and several were killed. We were thoroughly searched, received a hot bath and delousing, interviewed and became official POWs. We were then temporally assigned to barracks occupied by the British. They were real nice to us, they welcomed us with hot tea and we each got a cracker with jam on it. It hit the spot, even if it was only one cracker!

December 29, 1944
We received our first Canadian Red Cross parcel today, one package for two men. Broyles and I shared one and we ate together, slept on a table and used the British fellow's pot to cook in. Our ration from the Germans consisted of one sixth of a loaf of hard sour dough bread per man a day, a spoonful of jam or oleomargarine and a spoonful of sugar. We got Jerry (German POW) tea once a day, (like dishwater but hot anyway) and British tea from our parcels twice a day. Twice while we were there we got a cupful of Jerry soup, which was usually made from barley, pea, turnip, or rutabaga. We also got cottage cheese and horse meat a couple of times. (It was the best and the largest ration that I had since we became POWs.) I also got a chance to write a letter home, something that I wanted to do since being captured to relieve the minds of my loved ones.

December 31, 1944
We celebrated New Years Eve under a lot better conditions than we did at Christmas. The British put on a show in our barracks that lasted a couple of hours. There was a small band, singing and minstrel acts. A stage (improvised from the tables) was well decorated with the words "HAPPY NEW YEAR 1945—OUR LAST ONE HERE." I hoped they were right and we would spend the next one at home.

January 6, 1945
Today the non-coms (corporals and sergeants who were the non-commissioned officers) were loaded on trains for a trip to an American non-com camp, Stalag IIIB near Furstenburg on the east bank of the Oder river. (Our officers were separated from us at capture, and the privates who remained would be sent to work camps throughout the countries occupied by the Germans.) We were loaded on to box cars again but this time there were

forty men per car. It was still crowded and you still could not stretch out to sleep. We had a stove in our car so we were quite lucky. I made melted cheese and sugar on toast on the stove. They were just enough to provoke my appetite but we fared a lot better than our previous trip. It took us two days to get to the Stalag. We went through Schweinfurt, Leipzig, and Frankfurt on the Oder. (We passed the bombed out ruins of the SKF ball bearing factory in Schweinfurt—not a wall was standing except what was the front entrance that carried the huge sign "SKF." It was as though it was left there in mockery, or a huge tombstone. It made our spirits climb as we saw what our planes had done. The Nazis couldn't win this war.)

We arrived at Stalag IIIB near Furstenberg on the east bank of the Oder river. Sgt. Bob Wood of Bloomington, Indiana and I teamed up together as "Muckers." We stayed partners, watching out for each other until we got back to the USA. He had been one of the rifle squad leaders in our company. We moved into the American compound and had to share the same bed until we could find some bed boards to make up another bed in the other part of the frame.

Life at IIIB was better than at the English camp. We got one Red Cross Parcel between Bob and myself every week and except for the cold cement floor and lack of fuel things were getting livable. Bob and I did not smoke, so we could trade all of our cigarettes for food. You could buy a loaf of bread for about four packs, a milk can of oatmeal for three packs, two cans of flour for three packs, a jar of jam for one pack, etc. I got two books and a pencil that I used to write my diary and a future plan book.

I learned what an addiction smoking can be. There were men who would rather smoke than eat. When rations became scarce as they did later, some of these men would go without food in order to get cigarettes. We had a whole barracks full of men with tuberculosis in the barracks next to ours. This was the result of smoking instead of eating. Jerry's soup and rations were about the same in all the camps, just the amount, quality, frequency varied. Here we got pea, barley, oatmeal, turnip, (ugh) and dehydrated rutabaga soups. The last soup was terrible. It tasted like paper, and had an odor you wouldn't believe. You had to be starving to eat it. It was like sort of an indicator, you could tell how bad off we were by how we ate that soup. I often wondered what it must have been used for; it couldn't have been in the German diet. Maybe it was for the livestock. We got cottage cheese, jam or margarine, with the bread as we did in the British camp. (The bread was similar to German Army issue. It was dark, almost black, very heavy and had a moist sour taste. I believe this bread would never go stale and last for a long time without any wrapping or special care.)

German Black Bread Recipe

This recipe comes from the official record of the Food Providing Ministry which was published in Berlin, on 24 November 1941 (Top Secret) by the Directors in Ministry Herr Mansfeld and Herr Moritz.

50% bruised rye grains, 20% sliced sugar beets, 20% tree flour (saw dust*) and 10% minced leaves and straw

"From our own experience with the black bread, we also saw bits of grass and sand. Someone was cheating on the recipe." Joseph P. O'Donnell, Robbinsville, New Jersey. (Copied from Camp Atterbury web page, 2/17/2001 We always thought it tasted like there was sawdust in it! But we never suspected that it was really made that way. The German population did not have our food supply and used a lot of substitutes as in their coffee (Chicory and ground nut shells).

Potato was often mixed into the soup here instead of separate issue except on two days of the week. Bob and I bought a blower to heat our meals or water instead of having to wait a turn on the stove when it was working. (If fuel was short, there was no fire. A blower can burn anything, coal, green or damp wood. It was much easier to find fuel for it than something that would burn in the stove. The heat was concentrated so you did not need a big fire to heat something up.)

Turning a crank attached to the large pulley on the left turned the small pulley on right that turned the larger pulley next to it that was attached to the same axle. This second larger pulley turned another small pulley attached to a blower can that had an 8-bladed impeller that turned inside the can at a high rate of speed. This forced air up through an opening in the side of the fire box. This was made by a POW from tin cans, pieces of cord, scraps of wood, a few nails, and a German Dixie cup. The only tool he had was a scissors, pieces of glass or a sharp metal bar. Pulley was made by putting the flat board on the crank and with someone turning the crank he would use the glass or other sharp object to cut the circle. Boards and nails were ripped off buildings, bed boards, etc. Only the German Dixie cup (German mess kit pot) was obtained from a guard through a trade of cigarettes.

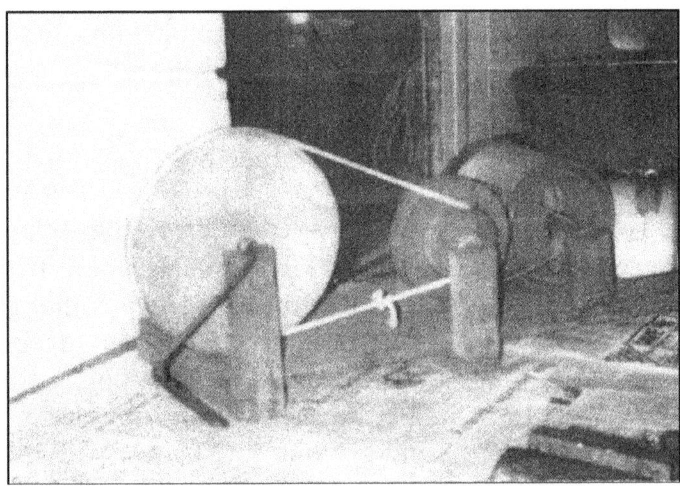

This is what a blower looked like.

Cooking was a team effort.

Contents of an American Red Cross Parcel

Box 10" x 10" x 5" (intended to supplement diet of one person for one week)

1 can oleomargarine	1 can powdered milk
1 can salmon or sardines	1 can chopped ham or corned beef
1 can meat and beans	1/2 lb. box of sugar cubes
1 can liver paté	1 "D" bar (approx. 1/4 lb. chocolate)
1 can American cheese	1/2 lb. bag of chocolate candy
1 can coffee or cocoa	2 bars of Swan soap
7 vitamin tablets	15 oz box of raisins
5 packs of cigarettes	

One of the popular dishes was a Stalag pudding. It was made from the crusts of bread soaked and boiled with raisins, sugar, and sometimes milk and chocolate. It was eaten cold or hot with oleomargarine and jam frosting. I made raisin turnovers while at Stalag IIIB and they were really good. I made potato pancakes that came out pretty good but they took too much oleo for frying so we could not keep making them. We really learned the value of food and proved it by using every crumb in some way or another. (In our trades we tried to end up with the most nutritious and satisfying food possible, for example milk instead of coffee or tea.)

Because of our constant hunger we always talked about food and home. One of the POWs that was bunked close by was Andy Dowden from East Hartford, Connecticut. He and I talked about visits that we would make when we got back home. (We never did them.) Here is an outline of what we plan to do when he comes to Torrington. He had one for our day in Hartford.

A Day in Torrington

12 pm - Dinner at Martha or Bertha (my sisters)
Sauerkraut + sausages + pork with potato pancakes followed by pies, twists and prune and fig turnovers.
3:30 pm - Stop at Krusers (German deli) for some baked ham sandwiches and pumpernickel bread, cheese, etc. and German pastry.
6 pm - Supper at ? House (Bantam, Thomaston Rd. or Winsted)
Home baked chicken with dressing, doughboys, cranberry sauce, and pies, etc.
8 pm - Stop at Toll Gate for an ice cream steamboat, milk shakes, etc.
11 pm - Spargilotti's for spaghetti and meat balls.
Have Hershey kisses and Nestle bars available at all times.
1 am - Home for Bromo and aspirin
(I can't believe that I really planned this, incredible!)

This is the menu Bob and I had planned for last week at Stalag IIIB.

Tues	Lunch	Turnip soup - Jerry
	Dinner	Oatmeal with raisins, toasted cheese on
Wed	Lunch	Barley or pea soup - Jerry
	Dinner	Potatoes, salmon gravy, Stalag pudding
Thurs	Lunch	Dehydrated rutabaga soup - Jerry
	Dinner	Meat and beans stew, toasted ham on bread
Fri	Lunch	Oatmeal soup - Jerry
	Dinner	Potatoes, salmon gravy, Stalag pudding
	Dinner	Potatoes, liver pate gravy, toasted ham on
Sun	Lunch	Pea or potato soup - Jerry
	Dinner	Potatoes, Jerry gravy made from Jerry meat
Mon	Lunch	Turnip soup - Jerry
	Dinner	Oatmeal, toasted cheese on bread

(Note: dinners would be absent without Red Cross parcels)

The menu was never followed as we were told that we must leave the camp. (The Russians were advancing through Poland.) It would have been the best eating we had yet since becoming POWs. I'm hoping that I get a chance to take Bob home with me when we land back in the States. Some real baked beans and all those dishes I'd tell them that my folks made, maybe he could sample them. Anyway we're going to have a feast wherever we land—all we can eat and split the bill. Ah me, on with the story—

January 29 - January 31, 1945 We were told the civilians are moving in mass through the town. Many of them are lying frozen stiff along the road side. We stayed in bed a lot to keep warm. When it would warm up a little we would work on the plans for our homes. The snow outside is about six inches deep.

February 1, 1945 We left Stalag IIIB at 6:00 p.m. last night. We walked all night on icy roads, really rough going. It was cold as we walked all the next day and I fell a few times getting a little wet. On the trip one POW was shot. We saw what looked like Jewish prisoners building fortifications. They wore long vertical black and white thin cotton coats. (They were digging though the frozen ground making trenches and mounds for gun emplacements. The men were old, very thin and sickly looking.)

We passed another group who were trying to run to the work site carrying shovels, picks, etc. There was a Nazi SS soldier with a bull whip beating the ones who were falling behind because they could not keep up. One man fell to the ground and he was beaten with a stick until he got up and tried to catch up with the others. Another poor old man could hardly walk and he was receiving such a beating I would have guessed he would never live out the day. (These were Hitler's supermen—beating up old starved and weak men.) Some of the POWS' loads must have become heavy for them because for they were dropping articles on the road. We picked up bars of soap, etc. that could be used for trading with the civilians should we get the chance. (Bob and I were always alert for opportunity.) We stopped at a large farm and after standing around for a couple of hours we found a place to sleep on the ground.

February 2, 1945 We walked all day still with nothing to eat from the guards. We ate from what we carried from our Red Cross parcel and some bread that we got by trading soap. We started out the trip with five bars and now we had none. The line of march was long, with hundreds in our group. We made the line stretch out longer than it should by increasing the gap between rows of men walking two abreast. We did this intentionally so the guards would be forced to spread out more. This then gave us the opportunity to stop to trade or look for something off the side of the road when we were stopped. If we were passing a field we would look to see if there might be a vegetable about, even a frozen turnip.

Passing one house a lady was standing in back of her fence offering about a sixth of a loaf of bread for a bar of soap. She made the trade to a POW a few rows ahead of us and then ran in the house to get some more bread. In her excitement she left all of her soap on the fence post; we picked it up as we walked by and traded it for bread down the street. (That's called "survival" under those circumstances.) That night we stayed in a barn where a Polish farm worker took care of us. He gave us some bread and sorghum and ersatz coffee in the morning. ('Coffee' was made from some roasted ground acorns, etc.)

The author spent time in several different stalags.

February 3, 1945
We walked from eight a.m. until three in the afternoon. Our guards gave us a fifth of a loaf of bread that was the first issue from them during the trip. The roads were loaded with civilians pulling, pushing wagons, some lucky to have a horse, all fleeing the Russians who were advancing through their villages and homes. They were all shapes and sizes like covered wagons going west. (Not quite; the pioneers would have appeared as if they were traveling like royalty.)

February 4, 1945
We slept in a barn again today. We received another ration of bread, one loaf for five men. Just think of how much people think of a loaf of bread back home? When I get home I'm going to buy a loaf of pumpernickel and eat it all by myself with thick slabs of butter on it, cheese, ham, and Polish baloney!

February 5, 1945
We "picked up" some potatoes at the farm we stayed at last night. (Bob and I found a storage mound made out of dirt in the yard. We dug in and found there were potatoes inside.) I traded five of them for a long carrot acquired the same way by another POW. It was good eating. Jerry got real big hearted today and gave us a loaf of bread for four men and a can of limburger cheese for eight. We stayed in an old chicken house in a deserted village used by the German Army for training maneuvers. We built a fire and made some oatmeal with rain water.

This an item that I was afraid to enter in my log. *(I entered date and code word to remember.)* While passing through a small town where Nazi SS soldiers were stationed, we saw a sight that told a lot about the heartless character of the SS. An SS Officer riding on a beautiful horse was showing off riding back and forth along the long column of POWs walking on the side of the highway. He wore a huge medallion hung on a heavy chain from around his neck that bounced off his tunic as he rode along. His nose was high and he must have thought he was Julius Caesar himself.

We were also passing a little house with a small boy (about five) playing in the front yard with his dog. The boy would throw a stick and the dog would run after it to retrieve it and bring it back to its little master, just like we have seen it done dozens of times in the States. One time the boy threw it too far and the stick came out into the road and the dog chasing it startled the horse who then threw back its head and broke its stride. The SS Officer upset by the dog causing his horse to lose its poise, turned back, pulled his pistol, took aim and shot the dog dead. Then he turned about and continued on his way, looking like he was proud of his achievement, teaching that poor heart-broken boy a lesson. I thought, how can they do this to their own people, a heartless, son of a ------ , he can't be a part of the human race!

February 6, 1945
Traded three bars of soap with a German driver for a loaf of bread. We also got our fifth rations from the guards so we did real good today. After another day's march, we stood around a couple of hours waiting for the guards to find us a place to spend the night. Finally we were moved inside of a German Army garrison and were told we could sleep on the cold concrete floor of the garage in the motor pool. (We had no overcoats, blankets, just our woolen pants and Combat jackets. This the way we left our lines when we left our combat position and this is all we had until we rejoined our lines in May. I often wonder how I made it through that winter, always cold, under nourished, yet no back problem, not even a cold!)

We traded some cigarettes for some sugar. We made a couple of thick salmon sandwiches with the bread we got the other day. Yes, we really did well this day as far as eating went. In the yard there were some captured American tanks. Boy, I wish there were American crews in them!

February 7, 1945
We arrived in Stalag IIIA just outside of Luckenwalde, about forty-four kilometers (twenty-four air miles) south

of Berlin. In eight days and a night of walking, we walked about ninety miles. This camp had prisoners from every nation that was fighting the Nazis including the resistance fighters from places like Norway, Italy, etc. We even had officers from all these countries in their separate section. As the Allies were advancing toward Berlin from both the East and West the POWs were moved into Stalags that surrounded Berlin. The camp was so overcrowded they had set up large circus-type tents to house a few thousand POWs.

We moved into barracks that were in a compound separated from us by a single barbed wire fence from the British on our left side. On our right was a double row of fences with a twenty foot space between it and another double fence both of which separated us from the Russians. (We were soon to learn why we were not encouraged to witness or communicate with the Russian POWs.) The British here look like living skeletons! Some of them have been here since Dunkirk. (That was around May 1940 when the English were pushed out of Belgium and the continent by the victorious Nazis.) The food rations won't be like it was at IIIB but it is still good to get off the road.

February 8, 1945
We got oatmeal soup today, real thick too. We got about five small potatoes and I am making soup out of them for our supper. They are moving 800 of the POWs that arrived here first to a camp that is seventeen kilometers from here.

February 9, 1945
Today we got weed soup and as hungry as I am I couldn't eat it. We made potato soup and thickened it with flour we had left. That and the bread ration was all that we had to eat today.

February 10, 1945
We got some good barley soup today. It had some horse meat in it that really made it good. I wondered what it would be like to eat solid food again. I know I'm going to appreciate what I eat a lot more when I get back

home. I think I'll be a fat man because I'm going to eat for a hobby.

February 11, 1945
We went to church held in the French theater today. It made us a little homesick but it was good to worship. I know I'll be a better Christian after this experience. It has opened my eyes to a lot of things I never knew or thought about before my capture. Our soup today was pea soup, real thick and good.

February 12, 1945
We had pea soup again today but I love it. I wish I could eat four 'Dixies' of the stuff. (A Dixie was a German army mess kit, an aluminum pot, about six inches in diameter and four inches deep. We each received one in a previous Stalag.) Bob bought a loaf of bread for a pack of cigarettes today and we sold half of it to our buddies Gaylord and Gabbia. We ate all of it; it tasted like cake. Tonight it's potato soup for supper.

During this time our Barracks leader asked me if I would serve as an interpreter with the German guards. He knew I could understand some German but up to this time I never let the Germans know this. I could listen in to what they were saying and tell the other POWs around me. So I agreed to give it a try. When I was interviewed by the German officer I told him my knowledge was limited because I studied a little in high school, not wanting to tell him of my German heritage. He said he would get me a book so I could study the language and I was looking forward to that; it would give me something useful to do. It never happened because a few days later, a new POW, an Air Corps gunner named Joe, had been shot down in a bombing run and because he could speak fluent German, I lost my new job. Joe told us that they knew of the Stalag here, and the air reconnaissance had followed our journey here from Furstenburg! We felt good knowing someone was looking out for us.

February 13, 1945
There was a black-out and an air raid last night and again this morning. They really are giving this neighborhood the going over. That's O.K. with me because it means that we are that much closer to the day when I can live like a man again.

February 14, 1945 Valentines day.
Are you still my Valentine Lil? That is the question that I am asking today. I hope she still has hope and feels the way I do. I wish I could send her roses like I did last year. I took out the letter I still have with me and read it over and over again. I hope the day isn't too far off when I can be with her. The good news today was oatmeal soup; the bad news was that our bread rations were being cut by a third. We'll be skeletons by the time we get out of here. This is Ash Wednesday and tomorrow we are going to have a Protestant service.

February 15, 1945
They caught a fellow stealing from another POW last night. There had been complaints by some POWs of items missing from their bunks for the past few weeks. Last night one of the POW's feigned sleep and caught his arm as his hand slipped under his pillow. A large shout woke everyone and the culprit was identified. This morning he stood in trial before the barracks chief (the top ranking sergeant) and he confessed to a number of robberies. First he had to read a prepared statement in which he asked everyone not to speak to him because he was lower than the most disgusting animal as he took food out of the mouths of his comrades. Then his head was shaved and he was made to clean the latrines for some specified time. He had to walk between two rows of all the POWs in the barracks who hit him with a bed board as he passed through them. He will face a Court Martial when he gets back to the US Army lines.

He can consider himself lucky compared to what some others got for similar offenses. In one camp a POW caught stealing had a rope tied around his ankles and was lowered face first into the latrine. He became blind from the lye that was mixed in the waste. I doubt if anyone thought about what might happen to his eyes. It may sound incredible to inflict that kind of punishment, but you had to be there to understand our mentality under our living conditions. Nothing came before eating—you can read it in my log of daily events, it goes on and on about food, sex was never discussed, just food and then getting out of there. I guess it could be called survival. Maybe that other group of POWs had even more hunger, or maybe it was because we were all going to church today.

I bought a wooden German carved pipe for five cigarettes. It will be a good start to making a carving collection. I took Holy Communion from an English Captain at the French theater.

February 16, 1945
Today marks the sixtieth day as a POW. Looking back I can say that I've really learned a lot during this period of my life. These have been the longest days and eventful days of my twenty-three years. (I had started my log book with the observation, "The hardest job in the world is doing nothing because you can't stop to take a rest." This was a reflection of the monotony of those long days of waiting.) Our cut in bread rations took effect today. Seven and a half men to one loaf instead of five men to a loaf. That translates down to one thick slice! We are now going to have eighteen Americans working in the kitchen so maybe we will get a better deal on the distribution of soup now. (Dream on.) The English, French, and Russians have been working in the kitchen up to now.

Saturday, February 18, 1945
We got soup two times today to make up for the cut in our bread rations. It was a flour soup and very thin. We saved the second portion and mixed it with some potatoes for our evening meal. Jerry (English slang for Germans) surprised us by giving us our normal uncut bread ration. Not a bad day. We heard that Jerry had confiscated our Red Cross parcels at Guben when we moved out as they did at the other Stalags that were

evacuated and they gave the contents to the civilians and Army. We could use a parcel real bad. I worked all day on my future home plans and they are beginning to shape up into something now. Guess I'll wash the dishes and hit the hay. (Dishes are used loosely here, they consisted of more like a hobo's eating utensils, tin cans, wooden spoons, etc.) Wish I could be home on a Saturday night date with Lil; let's hope it won't be too much longer now.

Sunday, February 18,1945
Went to the Church of England service conducted by the English Chaplain this morning. We got a quarter of a loaf of bread today—boy that was really OK. The bread tastes more like cake every day especially when you put margarine and a little sugar on it. I worked all day on my post war plans giving me something to do. We just had an air raid that lasted about an hour and now the lights are back on. I got a little sleepy lying in the dark but I am resolved to keep this log going. Lights will be going out soon for the night so I got to get ready for the night now. I'd like to have a Dagwood sandwich right now of toasted cheese, fried egg, baked Virginia ham, roasted peppers, cheese and relish and sweet pickles too. Oh me, someday, someday. . .

February 19, 1945
Nothing very exciting today. I spent most of the day working on my booklet of post war plans and talking about them with Bob and Gwen. I started the day with walking around the compound five times—real invigorating. Lights just went back on again after what is becoming the usual nightly air raid alert. Soon it will be time for them to go off for the night. The kitchen got a load of cabbages this afternoon so it looks like it will be cabbage soup tomorrow. That's all for tonight, so its off to steaks and Dagwood sandwiches in dreamland.

February 20, 1945
Last night was a busy one for Jerry. Air raid after air raid, it sounded like thunder coming from the north. (Berlin and Potsdam.) I had a nice dream though; we got

married again. If you only knew how many times this makes it now, Lil. I guess you are the one. We bought some French cigarettes from our guard and some tobacco that looks like it might be Turkish. I tried smoking some in my German pipe but it was too strong. Bob or Gaylord couldn't smoke it either. It reminded me of the strong tobacco called Trumps that my father smoked in his corn cob pipe. I don't feel very much like sitting up right now so I think I'll lie down. Wish we had some bread to kill that taste; it's wicked. Ah me, what a life.

Wednesday, February 21, 1945
(Our barracks were constructed with the wash room in the center dividing the building into two large rooms.) They moved the Americans out of the back room of our barracks today to the tents. Then they moved in some Italian working POWs. They are a dirty lot, using the wash room for a latrine for instance. The air raids went on all last night and some of the bombs fell so close we could feel the vibrations and see the flares dropping from the sky. One of the bombers came right over the barracks. Thank God he didn't drop any of those eggs accidentally. Ten men had to leave our barracks today to the tents to make room for some POWs that became sick down there. We drew cards to determine who would be the ones to go. When it became my turn two cards were left for me to draw from. One was the joker being the one to go—I drew the king of spades! Boy, what luck. I celebrated by eating some Stalag cake with some liverwurst.

Flash—this your latest news bulletin from BBC.

I am inserting an item that I did not dare write about while I was a POW. In this Stalag we got the news every day by radio from the British Broadcasting Corporation and the Armed Services Network. The British POWs who were across the fence in the next compound had built a small secret room under the concrete floor. Our barracks were built on posts about three feet above the ground so they could be easily inspected for any attempts to dig a tunnel. The washroom was built with a concrete floor on the ground and they did not suspect that anyone would be able to break through it without special tools.

The British however found that if they lifted the drain cover in the floor they were able to let one of their POWs down the drain. Then he was able to knock a hole in the side and start to excavate the hole and eventually make it large enough to crawl into it. The concrete floor made an excellent ceiling. To remove the dirt and not stop up the drain system they sewed up small bags that they could hang in their trouser legs. They would then walk outside and at the appropriate outdoor locations pull a string that would dump the dirt as they walked. Some of the dirt was dropped in the latrine from bags carried under their jackets.

The British had been at this location since Dunkirk, in 1940. Some of them had purposely volunteered to work in non-war related jobs in the town such as bakeries, tailor shops, repair shops, etc. Over time they had made friends among the Germans and using cigarettes, chocolate, soap, and other items from their Red Cross parcels they were able to acquire items from their German friends. Given a shopping list from the POWs that knew how to build a short-wave radio they acquired the tools and parts piece by piece to build a radio.

During the day, others would study the exposed wiring in the barracks and plan how they could salvage a piece of wire by changing the routing of the wire paths. At night after the power was cut off, they would then rewire to salvage the piece of wire. Eventually and with other purchased wire enough was spliced together to hook up to the radio in the room below the washroom floor. The German guards never were able to find anything amiss and this was going on long before we came to their Stalag. Early each morning a POW would go down to the room, the wire was hooked up, and he would write up the news from the BBC broadcast.

After the news was read in their barracks it would be passed though the fence to us and we would hear it read in late morning or early afternoon. While the news was being read we took extensive precautions to be sure we were not being observed. We had POWs posted at the doors and windows as lookouts. At any movement of a guard approaching the barracks the lookout would shout Air Raid. The reading would stop and everyone would appear as they normally would. As soon as the danger passed the lookout would say ALL CLEAR and the reading would resume.

The highest ranking and most senior sergeant in each barracks was the barracks commander. This was the line of communication from the guards to us and he was our leader. Our barracks commander had a map of Germany. I have no idea where he got it or how long he had it. At each reading of the news he would mark in the location of Allied positions. So we knew where the lines were on both the Eastern and Western front every day. What a morale-builder that was. It also became very useful to us when we later were liberated by the Russians. After the reading of the news the paper was burned.

Thursday, February 22, 1945
During the air raid last night, I was coming back from going to the latrine when I saw cluster flares dropping from the sky in the direction of Berlin. After watching for a while slowly walking on my way to toward the barracks, I heard a loud boom and I turned back to see if I could get a look. The guard stopped me and pointing to the door said, "Da ist der tier" (There is the door). I laughed and said to him, "Ya, und da ist Berlin" pointing in the direction of the blast. Funny thing, he didn't like me saying that! I spent the most of the day talking to Wen about college and to Johnson about barbecues. We got two forms for letters and a card that we can put in the mail this week. We got some fair chow—what there was of it—pea and cabbage soup and some salami. Two days in a row we got a meat issue; something must be in the air besides our Air Force. It's about time for another raid, lights will be going out, so *Let 'em have it boys!*

Friday, February 23, 1945
I spent the day writing letters. I got three letter forms and a card so I wrote to Lil, Martha, Ady, and J.B. Maylott. (General Secretary of the Torrington YMCA, a good friend.) I spent the rest of the time in bed, day-dreaming of school and what I'll need when I become a good

civilian. It was a dismal day and the soup was THIN. Outside of that nothing special happened.

Saturday, February 24, 1945
I spent the day as usual, day dreaming. I can't wait to get back and start doing some of these things. The soup today was really wicked. It smelled like limburger cheese and I told myself that was what it was and ate it. I'm still alive, I guess it was OK. They say the hardest job in the world is doing nothing—because you can't stop to take a rest!

Sunday, February 25, 1945
It was really cold today so I spent most of the time in bed to keep warm. I got an extra letter form so I wrote home. I tried to go to church this afternoon but we were late and the guard on the outer gate wouldn't let us go out even though our old chaplain was one of the group. Guess these Nazis don't believe in religion. I made my usual potato soup for supper. I put a couple pieces of bread in with it to thicken the soup, that way I can add more water so I can make more. Air raid came right on schedule, I guess it must be like a bus run for the boys upstairs. Wish I could be up there with them. It was a clear day and we were outside near the gate with our interpreter, Joe, who was talking to the German guard. We watched the sky darken with what was one of the 1000-plane daylight raids on Berlin. The guard must have been in his sixties or even older and he had bags under his eyes from the lack of sleep. He had a long coat that looked like it was from the First World War. He lived in Luckenwalde and he went home each night to his wife. He was a very worried man and didn't get much sleep.

It was near noon and you could almost set your watch as the planes were coming every day at exactly the same time, almost as though they were defying the Luftwaffe to stop them. Another indicator of their arrival was the taking off of fleeing German aircraft about a half an hour before the Flying Fortresses arrival to avoid being caught on the ground. The guard was telling Joe what a terrible thing the bombing was doing to Berlin, all the women and children being killed, etc.

Joe agreed with him saying, "You know they are all gangsters up there. You know Al Capone?"

The guard nodded.

"Well he was made their General." As the first formation approached us in their vee formation Joe continued, "Do you see the first plane in front, he is the leader, pray for him!"

"Why should I pray for him?" was the reply, "You said they are all gangsters didn't you?"

"Ah yes, but he is the only one with the map, you don't think they could have so many maps do you? If he gets shot down then the rest don't know where to go! Then they would have to drop their bombs wherever they saw a German. They don't care, women, children, long as they kill Germans. They are gangsters aren't they? You know in America everything is big sports. Well they make this bombing a sport too, they keep score on how many Germans they kill each time they go out. If they knew how many Germans were in this Stalag, Boom they would drop their bombs right here."

"Oh no, not on you, you are Americans here."

"What do they care, they kill Americans back home too, don't they? Pray for him. I tell you, pray for him!"

We had to go away because we couldn't contain ourselves any longer. We laughed as we saw the guard look up as each formation turned on our camp for its bombing run over Berlin. We could almost see him praying that the first plane doesn't get hit.

Monday, February 26, 1945

Life is getting real monotonous. Since I finished my Post War plan booklet, time goes so very slow. I wish I had some kind of book like math to study and do problems. I think about school and a lot of the details, just waiting for the war to end now. I'm really getting thin; my pants twist right around me and not so long ago I didn't need a belt.

Tuesday, February 27, 1945
Saw an interesting sight today, how Jerry gets a suction to pump out the latrine well. He drives up with a horse drawn tank carriage riding on rubber tired wheels. The latrine is built on a raised hill and the tank wagon is below the bottom of the well. First he attaches the hose to the top of the tank and the lowers the other end into the well. On the top of the tank there is what looks like a manhole cover with a spring loaded hinge to keep the opening tightly shut. Near the driver's seat was what appeared to be a valve and he inserted the tip of what looked like a spray gun. He pumped this gun that looked like a bicycle pump three times, injecting some kind of an inflammable liquid spray like benzene. Then he dropped a lit match through a second opening and there was a loud bang with the manhole cover swinging open and the fire shooting out to the sky. Then almost instantly the manhole cover slammed back shut and the large hose stiffened as the contents of the latrine well began to flow into the tank. Having started the flow the siphoning action to the lower tank wagon continued until it was full and he pulled up the pipe. Leave it to Jerry to think that one up. The contents were spread on nearby fields as fertilizer.

Wednesday, February 28, 1945
I had a blackout today. Wen and I were on a detail to pick up the soup for our barracks. We were standing by the kitchen door waiting for the soup to be picked up and after standing a while I collapsed and fainted away. When I awoke I found myself being carried back to the barracks. The medic said it was exhaustion. I couldn't see how that could be as I was lying on the bed the last two days. We better get some Red Cross parcels pretty soon. Wen and I played chess today and some cards. I had some delicious soup for supper, potatoes, bread, and cabbage. It tasted like a bean soup.

Chapter Four

Red Cross Parcels arrive

Thursday, March 1, 1945
We got news that we are to get some Red Cross parcels tomorrow Four men to a parcel. The French got nine carloads today and refused to give any to us. Joe Guspari, our conference man, with the English representative got the Germans to take three carloads and turn them over to us on the grounds that American goods can be confiscated for American use according to the War department. Our opinion of the French sinks lower every day. Whenever a delivery was made to the English or Americans we shared the parcels with the whole camp regardless of nationality. We were supposed to be Allies!

Only the Russians were left out because the Germans refused to let us give them anything. They said the Russians do not recognize the Geneva Convention and do not allow the Red Cross to aid their prisoners in Russia, so they were treating the Russians the same way. The British warned us not to tell anything to the French as they could not be trusted. They told us that the British had almost completed an escape tunnel when a Frenchman told the guards. They would not hesitate to do anything if they could benefit from it. Some of the French could be let loose in Germany and they would get along fine with the Germans. Fortunately our neighbors were the British, Russians at a distance, and Italians for a short period so our direct contact with them was practically non- existent. It was a dismal day, wanting to rain. We got a loaf of bread for 6 1/3 men, pretty rough. As yet we have no lights tonight.

Friday, March 2, 1945
A civilian walked into our barracks today. It turned out to be Max Schmeling, the famous former heavyweight champion boxer. He asked about Joe Louis and wondered if he was in the Army. Max was a paratrooper and was

shot up in the legs, so he is a civilian again, but still a German! He talked with us for about fifteen minutes and gave us packs of Lucky Strike cigarettes and then continued his tour. Now how could he have access to American cigarettes? That was a question unanswered but an indication that even in a war torn economy like Germany, anything is possible if you have the right connections and the money. We had a couple of daylight air raids and it's about time for their night time visit now.

Saturday, March 3, 1945
We had air raids again this morning; its getting to be an around the clock schedule. Glad I'm not in Berlin. I mended my socks today, a crude job but at least the holes are gone. Played chess with Wen again, even beat him for a change. Soup was good today, not very much but there were peas, barley, and some meat in it. Can't wait for some good chow though—

Sunday, March 4, 1945
I took a sponge bath today—in ice cold water. I shook every minute but I had to wash. I was just getting icky from the loose skin etc. We went to the Chapel Service which Dick Grey held next door. We met Kisel there, he had his hand shot up pretty bad and spent some time in a Berlin hospital. He said that about all that was left of Berlin were walls. We got good soup and seconds on this first day the American cooks made the soup. We also got a good quarter loaf of bread too.

Monday, March 5, 1945
We drew our first Red Cross parcel in this location today. We are supposed to get the rest of our allotment Thursday. So Gaylord and Gabbia are keeping this box and Bob and I will get ours on Thursday. Rumors are flying heavy today about everything from moving out to war news. I'm on fire guard tonight from 9:00 to 10:00 p.m.

Tuesday, March 6, 1945
We had a terrific air raid last night, the sky was lit up all around us. It lasted about six hours that I know of.

Rumor has it that a truce will be declared and we will be moved to a neutral country. It's too good to be true but never the less it is still pretty strong. We just got our soup cooked before the lights went out today. I'm supposed to go to the delouser tomorrow. I'm really looking forward to it, I need a bath bad.

Wednesday, March 7, 1945
It's a beautiful morning, cold but nice and bright. I got a haircut yesterday from an Italian barber. Boy was he good! He did a beautiful job in half the time a PX barber could scalp you. We had a lottery again today to see who was going to the tents. I got a reprieve again today. Whew—I hate those draws. **Twenty-five Carloads of Red Cross Parcels Came In TODAY!** This means we will get ONE box per man. We divided the box that Gaylord and Gabbia got Monday between the four of us and we had some real good sandwiches and a cup of good hot chocolate.

I just can't seem to stop eating. I'm forcing myself to lay off so I wont get sick. The sandwich I had with the cocoa was a fried ham and cheese with a lot of butter fried into the bread. I'm having a meat and vegetable soup for supper tonight. We didn't go to the delouser today so I just hung up my blankets and tick outside for a good airing. Supper was great—good soup followed by a thick slice of bread with butter and jam. I'm eating sugar coated raisins for a desert as we are supposed to draw our parcel tomorrow. It's hard to stop eating as we crave those foods so much. It's been a great day all right—just like Christmas.

Menu

6:30 am Tea (Jerry)

8:00 am Hot milk

10:30 am Bread, cheese and ham

12:30 pm Pea Soup (Jerry) Fried ham and cheese, bread, jam, cocoa

5:30 pm Vegetable and bean soup, bread and jam.

Thursday, March 8 to Wednesday, March 14, 1945
During this period I've been so busy that I didn't have time to keep up my log. The main reason was the arrival of the Red Cross parcels and the constant cooking and hot drinks that followed. We drew a box per man Thursday the 8th and then another box per man on Monday the twelfth. I've been going around trading items like coffee for milk or cheese with pretty fair luck. Bob and I continue to pool our resources and we try to eat those items that are the most nourishing. We both don't smoke and share the same tastes. As a result I have been having a lot of milk to drink.

I went to the delouser last Saturday and after the hot bath (shower) I felt real good. Wen, Johnson, Gaylord, Gabbier, Bob and I had a good supper Monday night. We had sardine croquets, toast, cheese potatoes, sardines and brown gravy. Hot sweet milk to dunk with an ice box cake that was Delicious. (Reading this now it was probably the Southern/ Louisiana influence of the other four that came up with that menu.) The ice box cake was made from crackers, D Bar (1/2 pound chocolate bar), raisins, prunes, sugar and milk. I've decided to include it in the list of things to have when I get home. (I never made it again.) We are talking about having three meals together a week. It is beginning to look like spring is just around the corner. Flies and other insects are starting to appear and we are getting a lot of rain now. We have been having a lot of black-outs too, right on schedule every night. The boys have been having their brews as late as two in the morning. All in all everything is just about as well as can be expected of a German prison camp. Time for that air raid siren now.

Thursday, March 15 to Wednesday, March 21, 1945
The first day of spring! It's a bit cloudy out and quite windy as March should be. We all had X-rays taken today, it took about five minutes. I made an ice box cake yesterday and it was very good. I used 3 crackers, 1/6 box of prunes, 1/2 D bar, 3 spoons sugar, 3 spoons milk and 2 spoons of butter. Next week I'm resolved to make three

real rich ones. That is one dish I have to make back home. Johnny was telling me how to make a good peach pie. Put a layer of peaches on dough rolled thin, then put a layer of dough cut in strips and another layer of peaches. Put on the top layer of dough, letting it sag in the middle. Pour on melted butter until the well that was formed is full and starts to bake. Almost two minutes before it is finished baking put marshmallows on the top and then bake brown. Oven should be around 110 for baking. I should remember to say happy birthday to Lil for St. Patrick's day last Saturday. Somebody else's birthday tomorrow, I can't just remember now! Oh Yeah? I wish I could be home to be with her—but it won't be long now.

We're saving food for a big Easter Sunday. It's going to be quite a day with a lot of good "essen." I saw Andy while getting our X-rays, he is living in the tents. I hope we get to go out on that big day back home soon. We built a table from a door and rebuilt the blower. I was accused of ripping out the door frame and almost landed a trip to the tents for pulling one nail out of the casing. I know who has the board so if anymore is said about it I'll be able to defend myself. Bread has been cut to seven men to a loaf and they miss some of our potato rations. I guess they figure we're getting too much to eat from our Red Cross boxes.

Thursday, March 22, 1945 – HAPPY BIRTHDAY LIL –

You couldn't have picked a nicer day for your birthday. It's a real spring day, just as warm as toast under Ole Sol's rays. Sitting here in the sun just makes me as dreamy as can be. Maybe some would call this Spring fever, but I think it is more likely homesickness. We could have a wonderful time back in the States today. Wonder what we would do? Take the afternoon off no doubt, go for a drive, maybe take a little walk and even do a little sunning like I'm doing now. We'd probably end up in Hartford and after a big dinner we'd go someplace to celebrate, like the Bond or maybe to a show if nothing else was doing. Then a stop at a milk bar on the way home and oh boy can I dream. Yes, we'd do it right but

> maybe 1946 will be more kind. Anyway it's a lovely day—no wonder, you're such a lovely person.
>
> I'm going to have a birthday cake—or rather a stalag cake—with my supper of fried potatoes and ham. I'd have made an icebox cake but we are short of D bars. It's coffee flavored with a creamed cherry jam icing. It turned out pretty good. Boy I can't wait to get home to have some real cakes. I wonder if you'll save me a piece of your cake today? Better not, it may get a little hard by the time I get around to tasting it. Next year I promise to make you a super deluxe ice box cake that will take you a couple of days to finish—unless you let me help you!!

This is another item that I did not want to record in my log. Each morning, and some times at an unannounced time during the day, we would be called to line up in formation outside of our barracks for a Roll Call. This was to see if we were all accounted for. The German formation is made up of five rows. They count the number of men in a row and multiply by five. The American Army formation lines up in four rows. So whenever someone was missing his buddy would tell the barracks leader and he would pass the word to line up in fours. The Germans never caught on. Their officer would shout at us, Dummkopfs, Funf, FIVE, DUMMKOPFS! Our barracks sergeant would go through the motions as if he were trying to get his men lined up correctly. He would move some men into the start of a fifth row. Soon other men would start a sixth row only to be told, "No, No, go back to where you were" and they would go back to four rows again. This could go on with the POWs acting more confused as they moved about, a real Academy Award acting performance. This would go on until the missing POW, seeing the formation, would get back from visiting the British or wherever he was. At some point when the barracks leader decided we pushed the Germans far enough and he would signal it was time to stop.

Then when we were in the correct formation we would hear a long recitation on how could the Americans ever hope to win a war with such incapable, stupid non-commissioned officers. We lacked discipline, couldn't be taught how to do something as simple as lining up, etc. Of course this bought us another five or ten minutes of time. Then the count was made, sometimes this would have to be repeated as someone moved to the right or left undetected. If it was determined someone was missing then the barracks leader would ask if anyone knew where the missing one was. The answer would come back I think he might be in the latrine or I think he is sick in bed. Often the person making the excuse would be asked to go see if he is there, another delay, and so it went until the POW finally got out on the field.

One might wonder how we could get away with this. The reason is the German training and how they view the military. What I am about to explain has been a fact that I heard from tales of World War I. The German soldier is trained not only to respect but to obey any order given to him by any officer without question. It is serious business not given to a sense of humor as in our Army. This mind set in the German soldier carries over to accepting orders from enemy officers as well. German POWs would not even think of the things we did. In American camps they would snap to attention, salute, and proudly march off if so ordered. They always behaved like the trained soldiers they were. This was one of the reasons that they lost some battles when their officers were killed and they had to wait for new orders before changing their battle plan. Hitler never thought that Eisenhower could make the decision to move troops on his own with the British. He counted on the delay that would come from waiting for Roosevelt and Churchill to approve the movement of troops. It was this quick Allied response that contributed to the German failure in the "Bulge." (This is documented in the US Army History of the Battle of the Bulge.)

The Barter System

"D-Bars for prunes, D-Bars for coffee, biscuits for cereal" these are some of the chants heard after the Red Cross Parcels arrive and the POWs' trading becomes more intense. Cigarettes and D-Bars (1/2 pound chocolate bar, used by Army for emergency ration) are the medium for exchange in the POW camp, or even on the road when doing business with civilians. Money doesn't have any value over here; offer some German marks to a guard and he will show you a handful of worthless *shise papier*! They want 'prima American goods," face soap, coffee, cigarettes and chocolate are the most popular items.

We got a whole loaf of bread for two bars of Swan soap on the road. All trades don't always come that good. It is like a stock or a commodity market, the prices will vary depending on the supply and demand and the persons need or craving. Here are some of the current prices for trades at Stalag IIIA; (pack means pack of cigarettes) D-Bar = 3 - 4 packs, Jerry bribe = 1 cigarette to a pack, loaf of bread = 6 - 10 packs, oleomargarine = 5 - 6 packs, coffee = 3 - 5 packs, Meat (Prem) = 4 - 5 packs, haircut = 3 cigarettes, Milk = 6 to 9 packs, shave, = 2 cigarettes, Raisins = 3 - 5 packs

Potatoes are being brought in by the Italians for 1 pack a Dixie (pot), and flour for 2 - 3 packs depending on whether it is white or potato. I was the Trader Horn, the one going out to look for trades. Bob would stay and trade with the fellows coming through. He bought the potatoes from the Italians for example. Bob and I would spend most evenings discussing price strategy. Items like what we had in our inventory, what we were going to need for menus, what we were willing to trade and how much we needed to keep based on when we thought the next parcels would be coming in. If we thought parcels may not be delivered and an item we had was in short supply we might hold on to it so we could get more for it next week. If we were able to find items below market value we would buy and hold for a price rise.

I developed a regular route of customers after a while based on what they were looking for and what they were trading away. In the next barracks for example there were a lot of fellows with TB and they needed milk. So I would make a trade for milk in another location, bring the milk to them for packs of cigarettes, coffee, etc. I also went over to the British compound to bring them tea and other items including potatoes. Some items traded several times and hopefully you ended the day with a profit. It was a way to spend time and Bob and I saw an increase in our food supply. It was here that I saw what a terrible habit smoking was. I just couldn't understand how some men would rather smoke than eat! They were so addicted that they would trade away milk and other nourishing food so they could have their smokes. Maybe that taught me a lesson too. It will seem funny to get back to the states where you can buy things for money and not trade item for item. What lucky people we are! Every American should have to visit a European War Zone to see what it means to be an AMERICAN!

Friday, March 23 to Saturday, March 31, 1945
During this period we've had some beautiful spring days. The sun was real warm and it made you feel like doing your spring housekeeping. We got the barracks good and clean today with a good delousing fluid sprinkled on the floor. I made a new friend over in the English compound next to us. Wen and I hung some blankets on the fence between the compounds and started to beat them. Then when the guard wasn't looking, we slipped through the wire to the English side and continued to beat the blankets a few times. Then we wandered off to look over the English.

While we were there, one of the fellows came up to me to ask me about the "Torrington, Conn." that I had written on the back of my field jacket. After telling him I was from there he told me that he had his RAF (Royal Air Force) training in Canada where he met a volunteer from Torrington. (Before we got into the war, some Americans went to Canada to join up in the British forces.) They went on a pass to NYC and then his friend got him a date with one of his relatives up in Torrington. He couldn't remember the names of the girls. His name was F/Sgt. John Watkins, R.A.F. of Middlesex, (London) England. After talking about Torrington for a while he said he liked my jacket and wondered if he could try it on. I told him I would like to try on his RAF jacket too, the jackets fit both of us very well and soon we decided to make a trade. So when I went back through the wire that evening I was in a mixed uniform. (I returned to the British compound many times on social and trading visits. John now lives in Canada, He fell in love with Canada when he was there, and we exchange Christmas cards every year.)

I tried a new dish that Wen talked about a lot, ham and rice with ham gravy. Of course you can't compare it to the home cooking version for mine was made with fried Spam and Spam gravy. It was real good so I'm including it in my list of dishes to have when I get home. I had three ice box cakes this past week and an ice box cake and rice pudding on Good Friday. We're all looking forward to tomorrow's big Easter menu. Johnny made the ice box cakes today, they look real good.

Easter Sunday - April 1, 1945
Well it's here at last. It's not such a nice day, cloudy, cold, and even a little rain this morning. I just got through with breakfast. We had cereal, toast with Prem, butter, cherry jam, stalag pudding and warm sweet milk. It was a good start on our Easter day. I can just picture folks back home with their new hats and suits going to church this morning. Remember all those colored eggs Ma used to color with spinach leaves and onion peals? Boy if I could only get back to those good old days. We went to church in the afternoon and then came back to prepare dinner. It was a big meal all right and the I.B. cake was super. I laid on my sack after finishing and for once since I was captured I can say I was full. It was a lot nicer holiday than last Christmas in the boxcar. We sure have a lot to be thankful for.

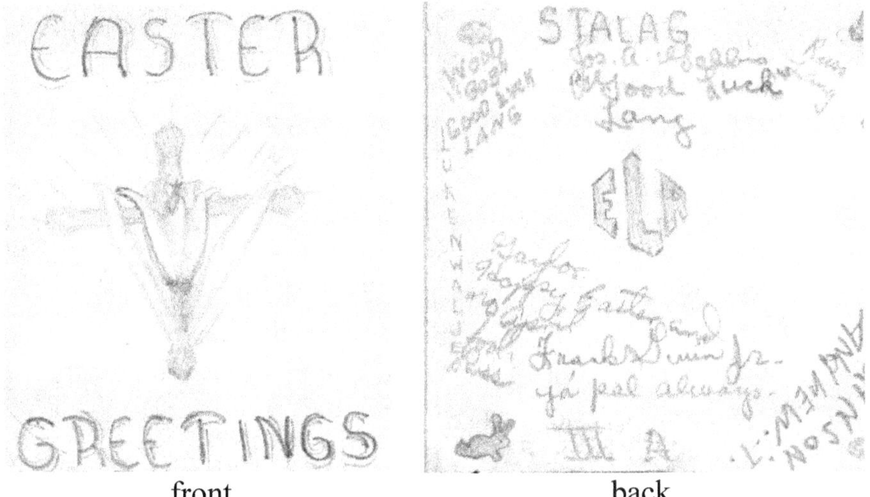

front back

This is a copy of the inside of the menu.

Breakfast Menu
Cereal – Prem –Stalag
Toast – Cheese – Milk

Lunch Menu
Peas Soup
Toast Cheese Milk

Dinner Menu
~Appetizer~
Meat and Vegetable Stew
~Main Course~
Fried Prem – Salmon Patties – Mashed Potatoes with Cheese and Brown Gravy
~Desert~
Ice Box Cake – Toast - Coffee

Monday, April 2 to Friday, April 6, 1945
The weather is behaving just like spring should, showers all the time. I think we have had a shower every day; they are just as regular as the air raids. Bob and I started to eat

together on a regular basis this week. We had good meals all week and thing seems to be working out okay. We made our second ice box cake this morning and we have the ingredients set aside to make two more for Sunday and Monday. Our menu has been the same as it has been for the last few weeks. Here it is:

Lunch every day was Jerry soup

Mon.	B. Toast, warm milk	D. Scalloped potatoes, toasted cheese
Tues.	B. Toast, milk	D. Perm, mashed potatoes, bread gravy, toasted cheese, coffee
Wed.	B. Fried toast, coffee	D. Salmon patties, salmon gravy, toast, salmon & grass, IB cake,
Thur	B. Creamed liver pate	D. Meat & Vegetable hash, Prem, toast, (never made the stalag, not enough bread}, coffee
Fri	B. Toast & toasted	D. Creamed salmon soup, salmon patties, ice box cake, cheese, coffee
Sat	B. Toast & toasted	D. Meat & vegetable stew, Prem., toast, toasted cheese, rice pudding, cheese, coffee (Never got the rice)
Sun	B. Toast & toasted	D. Prem., L.P. or prem. gravy, mashed potatoes, or rice, Ice Box cake, cheese, coffee

We've been deloused last Wednesday after one attempt on Tuesday. A fire broke out in the gas chamber and several of the boys' belongings were lost. The Germans gave them some Serb uniforms to wear. With Italians in the back section of our barracks, my RAF jacket, these

Serb uniforms—the place looks like an International barracks. Bread ration has been cut to ten men to a loaf. It's a good thing we have been getting the Red Cross parcels or we would really be hurting.

Saturday, April 7 to Saturday April 14, 1945
It's been a very good week. Our menu worked out pretty good with the help of some unclaimed personal parcels that were given out. We had a meal of chili con carne that came in the parcel last Tuesday. Then with some cigarettes that we got in our Red Cross parcels we were able toward the last of the week to make some deals. Bob bought up some rum extract and we made a pack on the deal when we sold it. We bought two Red Cross boxes full of raw potatoes last night and a couple of dixies (pot) of cooked ones. We had a darn good meal of mashed potatoes, Prem and gravy. It was the best meal we had since Easter. We had our usual ice box cake in bed and it was just as good as ever. Last Wednesday we were able to make a deluxe one with figs and dehydrated peaches that we got from the parcels. This morning we had a plate full of potato pancakes that were "prima." Tonight we are having the same menu as last night with beets added. As far as eating goes, were doing swell these "last" few days at Stalag IIIA.

I say "last" for the first time in this book for it's no secret anymore that the War is coming to an end. The Jerries all admit it and even tell us it is only a matter of days. We can hear the artillery fire, the P-38's and P-47's were overhead yesterday diving around bombing the towns. I was talking to the German guard out by our gate today and as a joke I said in German, "Postum, what is that thunder I hear? The sun shines and yet it thunders. Vas ist loss?"

He laughed and said, pointing to the open fields, "They are playing billiards over there."

The artillery rumbled again and I said, "See there it is again."

He laughed again and said, "You know it is not someone farting, you know darn well what it is."

A Russian work group came by and one of them carrying some wooden tree branches wanted to sell me some at a high price. When he was gone, I told the guard that he was like a "Chicago gangster." He agreed and said they have gangsters in Berlin too! How true, how true. Two Englishmen were killed and one wounded when they tried to escape during an air raid last night. Commenting on this the guard said, "You English and Americans are crazy trying to escape when you know the war will be over in eight days." Jerry has changed his views toward the American prisoners greatly these past few weeks. It seems hard to believe we will be free soon, but there must be truth in all these reports for everything seems to coincide.

Bob and I really ate tonight. I'm hurting and for a while I thought I might get sick. Bob peeled too many potatoes to fit in the Dixie. We fried them up, then with the potato pancakes for breakfast, Prem, toasted cheese for lunch before roll call and barley soup about noon, it's no wonder that I feel the way I do. It's fun feeling this way for a change instead of being hungry as we have been so many times. Yes, I don't think I could take a bite of ice box cake right now even on a bet!

Sunday, April 15, 1945
Ice box cake day, what a pip we made this morning. Bob and I should make someone good "wives" someday. We are rapidly becoming proficient in the art called cooking. For breakfast we each had about seven potato pancakes with a rum flavored syrup that was great. Breakfast was hardly over and our ice box cake made when we "brewed up" and had a "Jerry meat" sandwich. The next thing it was noon and dinner time so we had our Sunday pea soup with potatoes and cheese sandwiches. I'll be fat at this rate! We had a special formation at which "Taps" were sounded this noon in honor of our beloved late president, Franklin D. Roosevelt. It was very impressive for a stalag and the boys really snapped to a sharp hand salute.

(Our guard thought that now the war would be over since Roosevelt was dead. Again it was an example of the

German mentality that now was equating our leaders with theirs. They thought our president was like their Hitler who kept the war going.) Last night we saw one of the greatest fireworks displays that I have ever seen. They bombed a small town near Berlin (I think it may have been Potsdam) about twelve miles from here. Searchlights lit up the sky along with the falling red, green, and amber flares. A terrific pounding by anti aircraft batteries sent up hundreds of exploding shells leaving small clouds of smoke mingled in with the vapor trails of our aircraft. Once in a while a searchlight would catch one of our planes and follow it across the sky like a spot light on the leading performer in a show. The footlights were even there supplied through the courtesy of the Allies in the form of the blockbuster exploding bombs. It was a million dollar show for us, one that Jerry did not enjoy too much I'm sure, for the price of admission was much too high!

Monday, April 16 to Friday, April 20, 1945
Moral was very high during this period, especially during the first part of the week. For then many of us thought it was only a matter of hours for our liberation. The rumors were too good to be true for we are still here and the week is almost ended. We have seen a lot of favorable activity though. We know the War is being fought near us as the towns around us are being constantly bombed and we can see fighter/ bomber planes diving and swooping down to hit some Jerry target. Even now the windows are shaking from the loud thunder of bombs falling on Potsdam.

Bob saw a German truck camouflaged with tree boughs going down the road yesterday just like we saw on the road on our trip here. I hope that I can write some really good entries in this log by next week. We've been eating good since the Friday 13th due to some good deals we made with the Italians on spuds (potatoes) and a can of flour. We kind of "shot the works" on Tuesday for we bought about a pound of steak for three packs. It was very good about the best I've had on this side of the Atlantic.

Our menu was steak, mashed and fried potatoes, gravy, toast, strawberry jam, raisin and cheese turnovers, coffee and warm milk. In our cut of the unclaimed parcels we got about a quarter of a bag of candy, some tea that we traded for coffee but lost the can somehow. We had four ice box cakes during this period, all par excellent especially one deluxe one to which we added prunes and cereal.

Saturday, April 21, 1945—"Der Tag"
TODAY was the GREAT DAY that we have been looking for such a long time! The day that Jerry dropped his guns and decided that farming was a much better job after all! We heard the guns booming all night and morning. About nine thirty this morning the guards were ordered to leave their posts and marched away from us, leaving us free men! The Russians in the compound next to us went mad and their hungry stomachs sent them out raiding food cellars and even tried to get at our Red Cross supplies. The officers who had been moved from their POW camp to our camp came up to our compound and soon we were an organized battalion. We posted GI guards and a much smoother camp was being run than when the Germans were running it.

Long before this day and soon after the American officers were moved into our stalag, we secretly were organized into companies with names of officers, that we had never seen, in charge of sections of POWs. This was in clear violation of the Geneva Convention on articles of war that forbade such an organization among POWs. It was done in the event that if Hitler tried to have us exterminated, or if the Allies decided to air drop military supplies with paratroopers to free us, we would be an organized unit and not a mob. As it worked out it was beneficial to have things under control when the Germans left us.

Dopey, our little old sleepy looking German guard had locked himself in the little room in front of our barracks when the other guards had withdrawn. When our new Captain May started his inspection of our barracks, he opened the door of the little room and found Dopey sitting there ready to surrender to the first GI that opened the door. He handed over his P-38 pistol and said he didn't want to fight anymore. He just wanted to see his wife and children again. The captain wrote out a pass for him. (I doubt that it had any value in the turmoil that was raging with the Russians out there.) He took off for Luckenwalde to spend the night with his family.

To our surprise the next morning he was back in our area to do any tasks that were assigned to him and then he would go home for the night again! This is a perfect example of the German soldier's mentality. Their training was to accept orders from ANY officer without question. Other guards were reported to have surrendered to their prisoners in the same way. Maybe they were looking for protection from the Russians.

Our GI guards removed the machine guns that were from the towers that circled the camp and hung white towels all around the outside fence. Flags from every Allied nation were flying over many of the barracks by nightfall. (Amazing how these items could have been hid.) As for eating—it was the biggest day yet, as it should be. We had mashed potatoes and milk for breakfast, thick pea soup for lunch.

We ate a couple of "dixies" of mashed potatoes with plenty of butter in them, with gravy, a can of Perm and toast. This was followed with a butterscotch pudding. Bob went out on a detail and came back with three Red Cross boxes full of potatoes from the German guards' supply storage. So for our evening meal we had mashed potatoes, mixed with plenty of cheese and milk, a couple cans of sardines and some ice box cake with warm milk to top off the day's eating.

Soon an SS unit appeared in the woods outside of the camp. Immediately they started to send ultimatums one after another, like all men must stay inside the barracks, and for each man caught with a weapon 100 from that barracks would be shot. The major would ride up on his horse, so very proud looking for some excuse to spit out his vengeance. So we stayed in our beds and let them have their little desires for we knew that their end was coming. After a few hours everything became quiet as they left—our troops were coming closer.

I was real full in bed and it felt good to think that we would be eating this way all the time. Bob sold a box of potatoes apiece to Johnny and Wen for "D-Bars" that we polished off in the afternoon. Counting the D-Bar in the cake I ate three bars today! No wonder I should feel the way I do. It was a great day and all we have to do now is sweat out the coming of either the Russians or the Americans.

Sunday, April 22, 1945— FREE MEN

"They're here!" That was what I heard when I got up this morning, rushing to the window to see the Russian recon-car that just pulled in. Russians and the English were so crowded around the car you couldn't see it. It had come in to take the Norwegian general and American colonel back to the Russian command post. After it left it ran into a German tank that was still out there and it had to scoot back to camp. The car did get away okay. About eleven o'clock in the morning when I was on runner duty, I saw vehicles approaching the camp. The first to arrive at the gate was a Russian tank followed by four more. Then came a convoy of American built trucks, Fords, GMC'S, Chevys, Dodges—boy they sure looked good.

The tanks proceeded to tear down the fences in front of the Russian compound while their cameramen were taking movies of their rescue mission. As the Russian POWs crowed around the vehicles one of the officers spoke to them. One of our men who knew Russian said they were told that the Russians were on the way to Berlin. The prisoners were invited to join them in the attack and those that came would be forgiven for having been allowed to have been taken prisoners. In twenty minutes those able to climb up on the trucks pulled out with the other Russians marching after them on foot, on their way to fight the Germans.

Tonight some of our officers slipped away to visit Luckenwalde. Of course the rest of us were not allowed to leave the camp. We heard the gruesome stories the next day of what they saw and experienced. It was a bedlam, Russian and French drunk, looting and raping. It was tough being a German tonight, yet some of their own fathers and brothers were doing the same in other parts of Europe not so long ago. Some of the American officers were so sick from what they saw they never left the camp to go into that city again. We decided it would be best to wait in camp for the Americans to pick us up. That may be three to six days from now. What a great day that will be!

Luckenwalde postcard—a souvenir of the author's

Monday, April 23, 1945—"Fresh Food comes in"
Today the promises of plenty of food came down from the Russian general in command of this occupied area. His promises are coming true for by nightfall those American-made GMC trucks were bringing in sides of beef, pork, and bags of potatoes. Other captured German vehicles were bringing in the "rations" picked

up in the surrounding German farms. The potato cellar should be filled tonight the way the trucks are bringing them in. To top it off they brought in about nine cows, a bull and three calves in those GMCS, so now we have a farm right in front of the kitchen. I can see the Russians don't fool around with long supply lines. They just take what they need from the poor civilians who are left after the battles. (That is just the way Germans fight their wars too. We and the English must be the only ones who bring our own food.)

A Russian journalist was in camp with a crew taking movies and he was just in time to see the English moving out the Russian bodies from their morgue. He asked what did they die from and got the expected answer, HUNGER. The Russians died so fast from malnutrition that the Germans had a shed in the Russian compound where they would store the bodies. They were stacked like cordwood layered between sheets of paper so they would not stick to each other. It must have been hard for the Russians to look in the windows of the shack to see their comrades lying there under paper. When they got enough bodies, the Germans would come with a bulldozer and scoop out a deep hole. The prisoners would carry out the bodies, lay them in the hole, sprinkle lye over the remains and lay down another layer of bodies until the shed was empty. Then the bulldozer would cover them up with the dirt from the hole.

Some of the dead were found in a part of the barracks used as a jail, and others in their bunks. They just didn't make it. We heard of stories from some of the Russian POWs of how they would not report their dead so they could hold them up in their ranks when they were counted at roll call. This was so they could get a little more of the rations that would have gone to these corpses! Jerry deserves the revenge that he is getting.

Monday, April 29, 1945

The Russians moved us to another camp today. They thought we would be more comfortable while we waited for the Americans to pick us up instead of being behind the barbed wire. It was a beautiful officers' training camp called the "Adolf Hitler's Larger" that was located about six miles from Stalag IIIB. We stayed there about three days and then hated it when we had to return to the old Stalag. When we got there we had to drive out the French refugees who had moved in before we got there. So the first night we had to sleep on the attic floor. The next day we fixed up a pretty nice room with a stove, beds, tables, chairs, and many other housekeeping items we found around the Larger. We spent most of our time there hauling up coal, and booty from the apartments and warehouses there. By the time we left we had a regular little home set up!

The supplies that the Germans had stored up in those warehouses were remarkable. You could find any kind of an item from a file to soup kettles. We had all kinds of tools, electrical equipment, pots, pans, dishes, generators, typewriters, large movie cameras, signal and sound equipment lying around some in their original containers. We found some Leica camera cases so we dived in looking for the cameras but none could be found. We came to the conclusion that the still and small movie cameras must have been stored in the one of the other six or seven warehouses that had burned down. That was just our luck we thought. It was really a mess. In many places there were piles of colored pencils, pads, delicate sound equipment that had been stepped on and smashed by excited or ignorant Russians. We GIs had a lot of fun scavenger hunting and playing with all these "new toys" in their new magnificent playground. It was hard to leave the place but we loaded our wagons with booty, and picked up two bicycles from the French. One of them we had to make out of the parts from three bicycles so it ended up with a small wheel in front that made it slant forward! So back to Stalag IIIA we go.

I had no entry as to why we returned to Stalag IIIA. It may have been for logistics, ease of feeding us, etc. or so that we would be back where they could entertain us with their USO shows. They had brought in Russian performers and entertainers while we there. Maybe it was the start of trying to have us become "communist sympathizers." Who knows what their motives were? One thing is certain they were trying to hold us with them as long as they could. When they first liberated us, they wanted to repatriate us back to the USA by taking us back to Russia. Then we would be sent though Siberia to the Pacific coast where we would get a ship back to the States. We got out of that one by knowing that the American lines were on the Elbe River, just about thirty miles away. We never told them how we knew that for that would reveal the secret British radio. The British didn't trust them either. We would never want to get lost in Siberia or end up being a toolmaker there!

I also wonder why we were chosen to go to the Adolf Hitler Larger. They moved the French out of the rooms for us. Was it because they liked the Americans for all the lend lease equipment we gave them like all those trucks they were riding in? I always figured they had a motive—the Russians are good chess players; they don't make moves for nothing.

We are discovered

Friday, May 4, 1945.
A few American POWs were walking on a main street in Luckenwalde when an American Jeep went by. It suddenly screeched to a stop, made a U-turn and drove up to the POWs and stopped. It was a war correspondent who was traveling with the 30th Division on the other side of the Elbe River. He asked if they were Americans and receiving the affirmative reply he asked them what they were doing here! They told him they were POWs from a camp out outside of town where we were being taken care of by the Russians until the Americans came after us. He had them get in the Jeep and show him the way to this camp. He said he didn't think the Division commander knew anything about our being here. He made his tour of the camp and was surprised to find so many Americans and so many sick that should be in hospitals. He took off to report his find to the Division.

Sunday, May 6, 1945—**Time to Leave**
Right now we are sweating out the arrival of some 90 GI trucks that are supposed to come to move us out of here! Twenty five of those beautiful sights arrived about an hour ago to take out some of the "krieges" (POWS) from the First and Second Battalion of the tent compound. Yesterday a fleet of Army ambulances from the 83rd Division moved out the wounded and sick who were to be flown back to the United States. Yesterday one of the POWs gave one of the ambulance drivers a piece of German issue bread with some oleo on it and he couldn't eat it! He couldn't understand how we could "eat stuff like that!" All the time, it tasted like cake to us!

While waiting I'll try to go over the highlights of the past week. Food has become plentiful under our Russian Allies' control. We have plenty of bread now with the six loaves we got from the bakery in Luckenwalde. We are actually getting sick of pea soup! It must be that we are getting to be spoiled Americans again. Thank goodness for that! We hit the jackpot yesterday when the GIs brought in some ten-in-ones and K rations (field rations). There are only sixty to seventy men left in our company barracks—the rest took off for our lines earlier in the week. We were still drawing our full rations, so we had plenty of good American food for dinner yesterday.

We made up one of our favorites, yup, ice box cake (it turned out to be our last one) and that was about all we had room for. It's great to be able to eat as much as you want and not have to worry where your next meal is coming from. Besides the American food we have loads of potatoes, sugar, lard, flour, and other issue rations lying around the barracks that we can't possibly use up.

Wen and Johnson took off Friday for the American lines. We tried to get out yesterday in a group with our First Sergeant but the Russians turned us back. Most of the company had left because they were getting tired of waiting to be picked up. A few hours after we had returned to the barracks, we found out that a convoy of trucks was coming to get us today and after reaching our lines, we may get to fly back to a channel port. So maybe we were lucky that we didn't get out after all!

THE WAR IN EUROPE IS OVER!

May 6, 1945
Boy I'll bet the people back home will be celebrating and whistles blowing now! It is news that doesn't surprise anybody but it is sure good to hear those words. Now if God will be with us in speeding up the Pacific War, everyone will be able to come home again. We have two radios in our barracks now and that is where we heard the good news. Right now we got some good old American swing music on and everyone is in the highest spirits this wonderful May 6th, the END OF THE WAR IN EUROPE! OUR GANG is GOING HOME! A double holiday for us! I never thought I'd see the day when I'd have to save some of my ice box cake for later and turn down a bread ration because we had no use for it! THE WAR MUST BE OVER! Well, that's about all for now, so *Bring on Those G.I. Trucks and Good-bye To Stalag IIIA.*

That was the last entry in my diary, but now here is the rest of the story. The date is still the same, May 6, 1945.

Chapter Five

Free at Last

The American trucks showed up right after we had completed lunch, shortly after I made my last entry in the log. They were from the "Red Ball Express," a famous all black supply group that did a fabulous job of bring up supplies from Normandy to the Elbe, many times under very dangerous conditions. We all rushed up to the main gate waiting for the loading to begin. Then after a long delay we were told to return to our barracks and wait. We did and soon a black driver came into our barracks with a message from his lieutenant. He told us that yesterday they stopped loading POWs after the tent group because that was all the men that the Russians would allow to leave. They said they wanted a signed order or some kind of receipt for all the POWs that they released. He said the Ruskies expected that this would come with Eisenhower's signature on it! He went on saying, so we went up the road and bivouacked for the night and came back now and told them the order was on the way but the Russians were not buying. He then said, "Now the Lieutenant says that if you folks want to wait for Eisenhower's paper work, that's up to you. But if ANY OF YOU are found walking the streets down in Luckenwalde, YOU ARE GOING TO BE PUT UNDER ARREST FOR BEING AWOL and put on our trucks. DO YOU HEAR ME? SEE YOU LATER.

Soon after the driver left we all poured outside and headed toward the gate with our belongings. The Russian guards were waiting for us and lowered their rifles at us and ordered us to halt. We were told to go back and wait, we were not permitted to leave today. The mob soon drifted back to their areas. Bob, Gabby, Gaylord, and I decided we had it. We did not feel that we should be now the captives of the Russians. Who in hell did they think they were, sitting there with our supplies, trucks and jeeps and—we were getting more angry by the minute.

It was a beautiful warm and sunny spring day so we walked over to what used to be the German guard headquarters area. We took our shirts off and did a little sunning. Soon we got up and picking up our belongings we drifted down by a brook that ran through that part of the camp. Pretending to be playing by the water's edge we soon came to some bushes, and we continued now hid from the guards until we came to the Stalag fence. We put our clothes back on and once we cleared the fence we rapidly followed the depression made by the brook until we were forced to leave it and get up on the road.

We started to run hard and there was a call from the Russian sentry to HALT. We kept running, a shot rang out with another HALT. We ran faster and another shot, but nothing hit around us. After a few more minutes all was quiet. One of us slowed down to look back and he said to us, LOOK! We did and there in the distance was the Russian sentry, waving good-bye to us!! They were just bluffing, he must have orders to scare us into returning but not to harm us. So we stopped running and walked into town. As soon as we entered the town, a jeep rolled up beside us and the driver said, "Take your first right and the next left and climb up on the truck." He drove off looking for other POWs. In a little while we found the truck and climbed up to join the POWs that were already there.

When the truck was loaded the driver drove through the streets of Luckenwalde while Bob and I were hoping this was real as we were still in the Russian zone. Our fears were soon relieved when we passed a few places where Russian soldiers were along side of the road and they saluted us as we passed them by. It was late afternoon when we came to the Elbe River. The truck slowed down to cross a pontoon bridge that had been put across the river to replace the German bridge that had been blown up. The GI engineers had erected a sign over the bridge, "Truman Bridge." Bob and I said Truman Bridge, who's Truman? We knew that President Roosevelt was dead but somehow never heard or asked who our new president was. You couldn't find any happier group men anywhere as we came off the bridge and were welcomed by waving GIs from the 30th Division. Soon we arrived at our destination and the truck pulled up through the gates of a former aircraft factory.

When we got off the trucks and were welcomed back, they led us to the showers where we first dumped our clothes and then enjoyed a warm shower with American soap. Then we lined up and got new clothing. I hated to lose my RAF jacket but I did save three brass buttons as a souvenir. After having a real dinner, we settled down and slept in real bunks again, the first since we left England that seemed like ages ago.

We were told that as soon as transportation could be arranged we would be sent to Camp Lucky Strike in Le Havre, France. There we would wait for a ship to take us back to the USA. Since we were located in what was a German aircraft factory Bob and I did a little exploration looking for souvenirs. I managed to find some interesting photos, an ID badge that belonged to one of their "slave" forced laborers, a metric micrometer, measuring blocks and thickness gages. After a few days, we became bored and learned that there was no plan for the move to take place soon. Maybe they were going to wait for the rest of the POWs to arrive. Bob and I decided we wouldn't wait any longer. The next morning we stuffed some extra rolls and food into our shirts. We went back to our bunk room and packed our things. We put the food into a small towel and tied it to a stick, hobo style.

We walked out the front gate and down the road a short distance to the west. There we stopped and started to hitch hike. Within a half hour a small truck rolled up to a stop and the driver asked us where we were going. We said Le Havre! He told us to hop in and we were on our way. It turned out that he was taking his truck to a repair shop close to Le Havre and when we told him where we were going he said he would take us there. We arrived in Le Harve that afternoon and were very surprised when the driver came to a stop at the front gate of Lucky Strike! What service—the GIs of the 30th Division were great to us.

We walked in through the gate and were led into the office where we signed in and assigned to a barracks and put on the waiting list. I received a pleasant surprise—I was told that I was now a Sergeant, that while I was a POW the Army upgraded the position of the mortar squad leader position. We were told that if we wanted a pass to Paris, we could have one in a few days. However if a ship came in while we were away, we would have to go to the bottom of the waiting list again.

Bob and I decided that Paris would have to wait—we did not want to miss that next boat.

Lucky Strike was an interesting camp. When our barracks that were made up of the new arrivals went to dinner, we were served chicken and similar light diets for most of the first week. The next week, we were introduced to the heavier red meats like steak. They had an eggnog bar open all the time and an ice cream bar. We could easily have gone to Paris for we were there about two weeks before our ship came in. Later, talking about it we figured they were in no hurry to ship us home because they wanted to put a few pounds on us in a hurry.

One day I was walking down one of the company streets when a voice called out to me, "What are you getting stuck-up, Sarge?"

I turned at the sound of the familiar voice. *Could it be?* I thought, thinking of Chief, of my mortar squad—but that big lovable Indian wasn't there. Looking down there was a pitiful sight of skin and bones sitting on the curb. I couldn't believe my eyes, "Chief? Chief you son of a gun, its you! I sat down next to him and we talked for a while about everything except how he looked. I didn't want him to feel the shock inside of me. When I left him my emotions turned to such anger I could have killed the next Nazi I saw. Later when I came back to see Chief again I ran into one of the POWs that was with him and I asked what happened, how did Chief get into such bad shape?

He said, "You know Chief, he's so stubborn and so loyal, he was always committing acts of sabotage. They had been assigned to work in a brick yard. In the mixing areas there was the large mixers the chief worked on and somehow every once in a while the machine would break down and they would find rags, pieces of metal, stones, etc. that had gummed up the gears. Chief would be taken away and punished, put in solitary with no food for days. We'd say, Chief they are going to kill you. He'd laugh and say, no they won't and in a little while he'd be in trouble again."

At last our ship, a Navy transport came in. We were loaded on to trucks and soon we were going through what was left of Le Havre. It looked just like it was when we came through it months ago. It looked like the buildings or I should say walls and rubble were in the same spots. The only people that we saw working were the groups of German POWs that were cleaning up rubble. What a contrast compared to our ride through Germany. There, the civilians in every town were sorting out the whole bricks and boards, putting them in neat piles and carting away the rumble to land fills. The side walks and streets were clear there and yet here it looks like the people are waiting for someone to give directions or have the POWs clean up for them.

The ride back on the transport was much more comfortable than the ride over on the Queen. First of all, there were the meals, three a day and not the greasy stuff with the tiny orange for desert. Now we were having good American menus with ice cream! We slept in hammocks in large open rooms with the sailors doing all the details. The two-pitch whistle would go off during the day and the orders would come over the loud speakers, "Sweepers, man your brooms." We would lie in our hammocks as the sailors swung their mops over the floor below and tease them saying, "Present brooms, right shoulder brooms, left shoulder brooms, etc." as if we were giving them the manual of arms. Course they would come back with teasing of their own about Army routine as well. We got along well though; often the sailors would come around to see if we had any souvenirs we wanted to sell or listen to some of our war stories. Time went by quickly and in a little over a week we pulled into Norfolk, Virginia!

We were only in Norfolk a few days, long enough to get a physical exam, orientations, and our orders. It was here that I said good-bye to Bob who was heading to Indiana. I was given a three month recuperation furlough after which I was to report to the Lake Placid Club in Lake Placid, New York for extensive physicals and reclassification. I was given my back pay that had accumulated while I was a prisoner, war ribbons, dress clothing, and train tickets to home in Torrington, Connecticut.

Bob Wood

This page is in memory of my mucker. (A POW term for your partner. It must have been a unique term used in our camp as I have found other POWs never heard of it!) He might also be called my buddy, my close friend, my partner, or even my "wife." (Not in the sexist term however.) And why not, when you think of the amount of time that I spend with him during every hour of the day and night. We sleep with our bunks attached, side by side and even under the same blanket when the going gets rough. We eat together, make deals, play, work, talk, listen, loaf and spend the whole day in an area that is less than an acre of land. Who spends that much time with his wife in normal life? Your "mucker" is the one who knows where you are all the time, is there if you need help, looking out for your welfare.

My mucker was Sgt. Bob Wood of Bloomington, Indiana and a finer partner couldn't be found. He was the platoon leader in the last attack we made before we surrendered that afternoon. I believe my squad was trying to send some smoke to cover their withdrawal when the sniper pinned us down,

Bob has reached the stage where he can even tell me what I am thinking about at times. We both can sense the presence of the other by the sound of footsteps or other similar little things. We probably know more about each other's habits, plans, and life than members of our own families. We both don't smoke and seem to have the same tastes. He is soft spoken, tends to be quiet and one who will not waste words. Just looking into his eyes or that slight smile speaks volumes. He has a good head for business deals as he suggests some darn good trades. He loves motorcycles, owns a small home even though he is still single. He is trying to convince me to buy an (Army) staff car when I get out of the Army. We've had some fights or misunderstandings but we never have remained angry for more than a few hours. I guess most of those times it was because of hunger pains that made us grouchy. So here's to Bob, a swell guy and a great friend.

At this point reading my notes from fifty years ago, I am at times surprised at the hate that I must have carried not only for the Germans but the French and Russians too. Now I have many German and some French friends that I have come to know very well. This is a good lesson on what war can do to a person.

There is one group that I know I can never forgive, because to me they were in a class lower than animals. They were Hitler's SS troops. They were more like a cult, bullies who acted like big shots as long as they had the upper hand—like a gun. In the Battle of the Bulge they committed atrocities like shooting the prisoners at Malmedy and then robbing the corpses and taking their boots. They also showed that they were not the effective soldiers they were thought to be. Even with the best and newest equipment that Germany could produce, they were a failure in not being able to achieve their objectives. They had the will, but their officers were mostly political appointees and did not have the skills of the regular German Army. If they had any success it was when they were in the rear of the regular Army whose soldiers were more afraid of retreating and facing the wrath of these maniacs.

It was no secret that the Regular Army soldier had no use for them. The SS were cruel, full of hateful propaganda, heartless, and not possible to have any religious convictions, Life had no value to them. They used people to bolster their own pitiful egos and self portraits of supermen. They were the worst of criminals. I can't think of a punishment that would be equal to what they deserved. God will judge their deeds.

Back in Torrington there was much joy and a few tearful eyes of joy as I was reunited with my family. Of course I couldn't wait to see Lil again. She was working at the Union

Hardware Co. My first trip out of the house was over to see her and her family and to collect some of her kisses that she had been saving for me!

Shortly after my return home, I went to our German Lutheran Church on Sunday with members of my family. While I was in Camp Lucky Strike near Le Havre, France waiting for transport home, I wrote some letters to my family and friends. One went to John Maylot, General Secretary of the YMCA with whom I had a long term friendship. By steering me into club work, and encouraging me to accept responsibilities by taking club offices at the local and state levels, he had turned me away from the shy introvert that I was when we first met. I was still filled with hate for my German captors when I wrote to him and said some very unkind remarks about the Germans. I thought it was just going to be a letter to him. He sent a copy of the letter to the local newspaper, the Torrington Register.

The Pastor of our church read it and remembered what I said. When I attended the service that Sunday, weeks after it appeared in the newspaper, he made a point of including some remarks in his sermon on that Sunday about hate that were clearly aimed at me. When the service was over and I was outside the church, several members came over to greet me and said that if I had left the service during those remarks they would have followed me out! I explained that no longer felt that way and at the time I wrote that letter I was still not over my anger.

The week days were long and boring, Lil was at work, most of my friends were still in the Service, and after all my visiting was done there wasn't much to do. I'd hang around the YMCA a lot talking to Jack Maylot, but I think after a while I must have been getting in his way too, although he would never say so. One day Jack asked me. "How would you like to go to work?" He told me that a leaf tobacco grower from Simsbury was looking for teenagers or anyone else to harvest his crop. He said my job would be to recruit the workers (I put an ad in the newspaper), bring them to the fields each day in his bus, and take care of paying them. His men would take over in the fields and I was free until it was time to see that they got back home. It was a six week job and I got a great salary and an equal bonus at the end of the harvest if I kept my quota at full strength. I did, and it was the most money I ever saw up to that point in my life.

It was a great summer, food was no longer the top priority in my life. I soon forgot all those plans I made for making ice box cakes or going on the tour of eating places I used to dream about. Now Lil became my number one thought and I spent as much time with her as I could.

THE WAR IS OVER!

August 15, 1945—after two atomic bombs, Japan surrendered and World War II was over at last! Torrington, like the rest of the country was celebrating, whistles blowing, church bells ringing, and partying everywhere. I went up to Lil's house, naturally, and we could hardly get off her street as we walked to go to join the celebration in the town's center. People were out of their homes kissing and hugging, pouring drinks and offering refreshments. After a few hours we returned home, the partying got to be too much and we were becoming ill from the effects of too much refreshment in too short a time. It was a great day, and I now could look forward to ending my Army career.

A few weeks later, my ninty day recuperation furlough was finished and I reported to the Lake Placid Club in Lake Placid, New York, for a thorough three- day physical examination and orientation sessions. I was reclassified as I-C, not eligible for combat duty. I was eligible to serve as cadre in a training camp. The rest of the week we were free to enjoy the facilities of the club and have a guest join us. I called Lil and she came up with another girl friend of a POW from Torrington who was there with me. Lil and (Mary?) stayed in a private home that was next to the Club that took in guests.

When Lil and Mary had to leave they took the bus back to Albany that was supposed to make a connection with a bus that would be going though Torrington. When they got to

Albany the Torrington bus had already left, it was the last bus for the day! They asked a policeman where they could get a room for the night. He suggested the YWCA. They tried but it was full. They called us and told us what happened so we took the next bus to Albany and stayed with them in Albany until their bus came in the morning.

I was sent to Camp Hood, Texas for cadre duty. It was a huge camp that was used to train Armored and Tank divisions as well as basic Infantry training. It was in the middle of no where but next to a nice little town called Temple. Temple was known for its sanitarium for the treatment of tuberculosis. The Army was discharging its soldiers by the point system. Points were based on the number of months you were in the service plus points for time in combat areas, wounded, POW, etc. Since I was short of the point level that was being released I was going to have to wait out my turn training new recruits.

When I reported in for assignment I noticed that some of the interviewing soldiers were wearing the same shoulder patch as mine, the Roaring Lion that represented the 106th Division. As my turn came up, one of the interviewers beckoned to me. I pointed to my shoulder patch and to the soldier at the next desk from my Division. He gave me an OK sign and I waited until the 106th Division soldier was free. After comparing notes, he was from G company of my Regiment, he looked over my service record and asked, "You don't want field duty do you?" I told him that I rather not and asked what did he have in mind. After asking about what skills I had, he shook his head and said this going to be tough but let's give it a try.

He sent me to the camp office. I reported along with another soldier to the Captain in the office. The Captain first looked over the soldier's record, saw he had typing experience, exclaimed his approval and told him where to report for duty. Then he looked at my record and then asked me if I could type. I said no and no again to all of the next group of questions that were all related to office work.

He looked up at me and said "Then what in hell are you doing here?"

I replied, "I don't know, Sir." Then pointing to my shoulder patch I said, "Maybe because they don't—"

I never finished. He looked at my patch and said "I'm sorry Sergeant, I should have noticed." Then looking down at his requirement list he said "Let's see what we can find, oh here, report to Corporal— in the IN and Out section."

I landed a desk job, checking service records of soldiers coming into camp and those leaving, to be sure all the entries had been made correctly and there were no omissions. What a soft job, reporting to a boss that I out ranked. I soon became a bureaucrat. I would come in to work when I wanted and leave early; the Corporal never objected. Because I saw who was being discharged I knew where I was on the list all the time. Just before Thanksgiving, I figured I should be on the last group leaving before the holiday. When the list came out and I wasn't on it, I went to the lieutenant and asked why I wasn't on the list. They were up to my number and had passed the L's on the list. He agreed, a special order was drawn up with just my name on it. I received my discharge and left with the other group. I was given a train ticket to Torrington, Connecticut and I was home for Thanksgiving.

Chapter Six—Decorations

Sgt. E.Russell Lang Army Serial # 31345144 Stalag # 312667. 60mm Mortar Squad leader, in Company I of the 423rd regiment, 106th Division, US Army. Became Sergeant (3 stripes) while POW. Awarded ETO Ribbon with three Battle Stars, American Theater Victory, Good Conduct Ribbons and the Combat Infantryman's badge. Left USA October 17, 1944 from Fort Myles Standish, Massachusetts via New York City on the Queen Elizabeth to Greenock, Scotland (October 1944) and then to Cheltenham, England. Left Southampton and arrived in Le Havre, France in December. Two days later we replaced the 2nd Airborne Division in the Siegfried line. The Battle of the Bulge began Dec16th and I was captured on December 19th. I was processed as a POW on Dec 29th in Stalag XIIA near Limburg, Germany.

Good conduct · American Campaign · WW II Victory

Prisoner of War
European ET with Battle Stars
Bronze star

Honorable WW II
RIFLE
MORTAR
ASTP Training
Sergeant
Rifle marksmanship

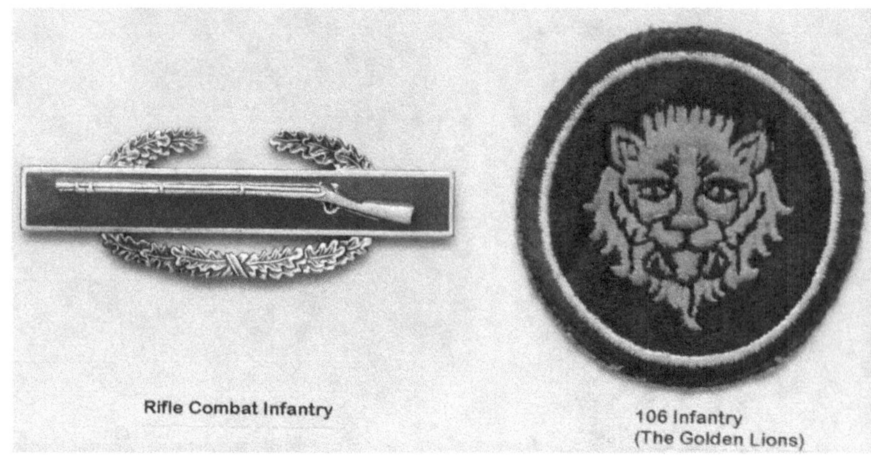

Rifle Combat Infantry

106 Infantry
(The Golden Lions)

New York State Conspicuous Service Cross

Top: Piping for Edge of Cap Denotes Infantry
Rifle in Wreath - Combat Infantry Badge
Brass Collar Buttons- Infantry and US Army
Right Side- Rifle Marksmanship
Ribbons (Horizontal Bars with Vertical Stripes)

Top - World War II
Left - Good conduct Middle - European Theater
Right - Ardennes with three battle stars

Army of the United States

Honorable Discharge

This is to certify that

ELMER R LANG 31 345 144 Sergeant

Company I 423rd Infantry Regiment

Army of the United States

is hereby Honorably Discharged from the military service of the United States of America.

This certificate is awarded as a testimonial of Honest and Faithful Service to this country.

Given at Camp Hood Texas

Date 21 November 1945

Howard L. Shinaberger
HOWARD L SHINABERGER
Lieutenant Colonel Infantry

Chapter Seven—Photos and Souvenirs

Personalkarte I: Personelle Angaben

Kriegsgefangenen-Stammlager: Lager: IVB

Name: Lang

Vorname: Elmer Russell

Geburtstag und -ort:

Religion: Lutheran

Vorname des Vaters: John

Familienname der Mutter:

Staatsangehörigkeit:

Dienstgrad:

Truppenteil:

Zivilberuf:

Matrikel Nr.:

Gefangennahme:

Ob gesund, krank, verwundet eingeliefert:

Lichtbild

Nähere Personalbeschreibung

Größe: 5' 11"

Haarfarbe: Blonde

Augen: Blue

Besondere Kennzeichen:

Fingerabdruck des rechten Zeigefingers

Name und Anschrift der zu benachrichtigenden Person in der Heimat des Kriegsgefangenen:

Father – 49 Wall St. Torring

LANG ELMER

My German POW Service Record

POWs at Stalag IIA, Luckenwalde

POWs operating blower in the overflow "tent city" at Luckenwalde

(These two photos were sent to me by John Watkins, my Royal Air Force buddy, now living in Canada.)

Luckenwalde in 1938

This is one of the photos I picked up after we were liberated. Two more are on the facing page.

Rally at a German Aircraft Factory
"1941—New Year, a new battle, a new Victory!"

At the rally, Propaganda Minister Goebels on the right.

Italian worker's ID badge I found in the aircraft factory.

10,000 Mark note. Picked up from the floor in a Luckenwalde office that had been sacked by the Russians. With the collapse of the government, the worthless money was left laying around.

1-12-45

Six From City Reported Missing On Western Front

[illegible]

May 26, 1945

Corp. Elmer Lang Notifies Family He Is Prisoner

[illegible]

Corp. Lang Returns After Being Prisoner

[illegible]

Discharges

[illegible]

June 7, 1945

Corp. Lang Tells Of Experiences As German Prisoner

[illegible]

(Continued On Page Fifteen)

Present view of base of the Schnee Eifel ridge held by the 423rd Infantry Regiment December 16, 1944. (Photos by Carl Wouters)

Foxhole remnant in area held by I Company.

View toward Schönberg from Hill 504. (Photos by Carl Wouters)

Schönberg in 2008.

Present day view of foxhole on Hill 504
near Schönberg. (Photo by Carl Wouters)

Index

J

K

L

M

N

P

Q

R

S

T

150506

www.ingramcontent.com/pod-product-compliance
Lightning Source LLC
Chambersburg PA
CBHW070626300426
44113CB00010B/1681
9780998361901